It can be hard to keep up with an out-of-control juggernaut f No sooner has one scandal rea crushed beneath his wheels, on., ... ---- while the country is dragged along behind, and no deal Brexit looms ever closer. 'There will be drinking water,' Johnson has promised.

Heathcote Williams composed his 'study in depravity' more than three years ago, before the 2016 EU referendum, before Johnson's careless talk condemned Nazanin Zaghari-Ratcliffe to an Iranian jail cell, before the police were called to a domestic dispute at his girlfriend's flat, before he said his hobby was making model buses out of old wine boxes. But Williams's portrait is as true a likeness of its subject now as it was then.

Drawing on biographies by Sonia Purnell and Andrew Gimson, a great many newspaper articles, and Johnson's own journalism and TV appearances, Williams assembles a blistering charge sheet: climate change denial, dishonesty, hypocrisy, incompetence, racism, violence, 'remorseless self-promotion', 'a ruthless and often cruel ambition together with an elitism and a ferocious temper when challenged'.

Boris Johnson may still be racking up the aliases – mayor of London, foreign secretary, prime minister? – but the only one he deserves is the beast of Brexit.

BORIS JOHNSON:
THE BEAST OF BREXIT

Boris Johnson:

The Beast of Brexit

A STUDY IN DEPRAVITY

Heathcote Williams

With a preface by Jeremy Harding
and an afterword by Francis Wyndham

This edition first published in 2019 by the *London Review of Books*
28 Little Russell Street, London WC1A 2HN
Previous editions published in 2016, 2017

ISBN 978 1 9996361 7 3

Typeset by LRB (London) Limited
The text is set in Linotype Janson Text
Printed and bound in Great Britain
by Clays Ltd, Elcograf S.p.A.

lrb.co.uk

CONTENTS

Run-ins with the Gatekeepers

Jeremy Harding

'WHITMANESQUE' is how Colin Ward, writing in the *London Review of Books*, described Heathcote Williams's book *Whale Nation* (1988), an epic hymn in verse to an animal then – and still – under terrible threat. Williams himself was a difficult catch. We tried to get him to write for the *LRB*, then lost heart; gathered up our courage, only to fall back again in despair. There are just two pieces by Williams in the *LRB* archive. The first is a poem – though there isn't much dolling up, and nothing conspicuously 'poetic' – which plays with the idea of wars as music festivals ('The music was mainly percussive... There have been several attempts to get the show on the road again'). In the second, a review of Roger Deakin's *Waterlog*, Williams follows the author and 'his trusty snorkel' on 'a swimmer's journey through Britain'.

Williams loved the free-form trespassing that Deakin went in for, in all weathers, in all temperatures (he'd been kitted out for cold by 'a wetsuit couturier'), in all waters, irrespective of fishing or mooring rights. He relishes Deakin's run-ins with the gatekeepers, especially when

he explores the River Itchen – there were few spots in England 'more fertile or pleasant', Cobbett wrote, 'and none, I believe, more healthy' – ignoring a Private Fishing notice, vaulting a fence along the bank, and leaping in, musing mouth-wateringly on Cobbett's description of a strawberry garden further upstream at Martyr Worthy, where maids supplied him with cream from a nearby milk-house. He is wakened from his 19th-century reverie by an irate porter from Winchester College with an alsatian, and an officious College river keeper, who angrily strut up and down beside him on the bank, affronted by the sight of his rubber-blubbered body in their watery patch. They shout out repeatedly: 'Does that fence mean *anything* to you?' Deakin insists, between continuing breast-strokes, on his self-accorded rights 'as a free swimmer', and ignores the warning that he is 'scaring away the trout' – exclusively reserved, it transpires, for Old Wykehamist fishermen. He surges on . . .

Williams himself preferred to be under water, beneath all the thrashing about on the surface. Underground, too, and there's no doubting he was a jubilant presence on the British countercultural scene during the 1960s, but once that moment had passed he flipped his flukes and sounded. There was no chat show banter, not much image-grooming. He became elusive, rather than reclusive; you only got wind of him in his screen appearances, most of them, unlike his Prospero for Derek Jarman's version of *The Tempest*, in modest roles. But the writing kept appearing. And his great play *AC/DC*, performed at the Royal Court's Theatre Upstairs in 1970 before transferring to the main house, was somehow self-updating: not so much the satire on radical psychiatry – hilarious and scary by turns – as the furious take on junk-information culture.

He wrote and published a great many scurrilous pamphlets,

sometimes unsigned, over the years, usually photocopied and ring-bound and circulated among friends. A copy of *The Blond Beast of Brexit* landed in the *LRB* offices in the spring of 2016, before the EU referendum, when Boris Johnson was 'widely judged to be the heaviest hitter' in the campaign for Britain to leave the European Union. Thomas Jones wrote about the pamphlet on the *LRB* blog:

> Drawing on biographies of the mayor of London by Sonia Purnell and Andrew Gimson, a great many newspaper articles, Johnson's own journalism in publications from the *Eton Chronicle* to the *Daily Telegraph* (what range!) and a few of his countless TV appearances, Williams assembles a blistering charge sheet against his target: climate change denial, dishonesty, hypocrisy, incompetence, racism, violence, 'remorseless self-promotion', 'a ruthless and often cruel ambition together with an elitism and a ferocious temper when challenged'.

As demand for Williams's broadside outstripped supply, the London Review Bookshop took on the publishing of it. The first edition was reprinted eight times. This, the second, is essentially unchanged (after all, so is Boris Johnson). The only new inclusion is a piece from the very first issue of the *LRB*, in 1979, by Williams's friend Francis Wyndham, which may go to show how much rosier things looked at the time.

Williams died on 1 July 2017. In his last year, following the publication of *The Blond Beast of Brexit*, he had kept up the good work. A volume responding to President Trump, *American Porn*, appeared in January 2017 from Thin Man Press. And *Royal Babylon*, 'an investigative poem' of 424 quatrains denouncing the monarchy – 'fossilised spivs', 'a life-threatening family' – was put out by Skyscraper Publications. Rough and ready is the best way I can think of to describe the Williams poetics: 'Yet true or false, paranoid suspicions are a predictable by-product/Of a plutocratic cult, still ring-fenced by force of arms.' Unlike the lyrics he wrote for Marianne Faithfull's 'Why D'ya Do It' on *Broken English* – a-b-c-b-d-d – there's not a lot of rhyme in *Royal Babylon*, which makes it all the more remarkable when we happen across it now and again:

It's clear that an acquisitive instinct is an endemic *trait*
In the British royal family's DNA

Williams may not have tried his hand at self-advertising, but he did the best he could for his books. The poem arrived in the *LRB* offices with a note inside for the editor: 'Harpooning dinosaurs... for favour of review, Heathcote.'

Boris Johnson

The Blond Beast of Brexit

A STUDY IN DEPRAVITY

Every violation of truth is not only a sort of suicide in the liar, but is a stab at the health of human society.

Ralph Waldo Emerson

Just because you *are* a character doesn't mean you *have* character.

The Wolf in Quentin Tarantino's 'Pulp Fiction'

You don't look right, never mind act right. Get out of public life!

Paul, brother of Ken Bigley, to Boris Johnson on the occasion of Johnson's ill-starred visit to Liverpool

IN ORDER TO SILENCE the dissenters within his own party and to silence those in Britain raising objections to their country being part of Europe the Tory prime minister, David Cameron, mounted a charm offensive; a mission to the European leaders in order to try to vary the terms and conditions for Britain's membership; in particular to reform Europe's position on its borders and to limit the free movement of its citizens.

Cameron's negotiations were in some degree successful, at least by his lights, and he was able to proclaim that Britain had been accorded a 'special status' which would allow it something of a free hand in its migrant policy.

However, this proved insufficient for some of his fellow party members – those who, echoing the words of John Major, might be referred to as the 'bastard' wing of the Tory Party – and, in somewhat dramatic circumstances, three of Cameron's closest friends stepped forward to decry their friend's offering and to announce that all three were now endorsing the aims of the Britain Must Leave lobby.

In an eerie echo of Shakespeare's *Julius Caesar*, the three effusively insisted that their leader was 'an honourable man' before concluding that the concessions which he had wrung from Europe were not worth the paper they were written on and that therefore they had no alternative but to knife their Tory Caesar in the Forum.

In the light of this upheaval, there is now to be a referendum in Britain on 23 June in which the public at large will be invited to decide Britain's place in Europe. In or out.

Since these mini-masters of Realpolitik, Cameron's would-be assassins, are likely to be the most loquacious in their advocacy of Britain's leaving and, since they may well influence public opinion through their prominent media presence, it's worth scrutinizing their credentials in order to judge their persuasive powers.

They are an unsavoury and often suspect bunch. Michael Howard, now Lord Howard, was once a punitive home secretary who voted for the reintroduction of the death penalty. In the words of his fellow Tory MP, Anne Widdecombe, 'He has something of the night about him,'[1] and she would later call him 'a gloating bully'.[2]

A prisons director, Derek Lewis, unfairly sacked by Howard saw fit to pass the following verdict on him:

'Too much of what he does is directed to his own personal political career, too little to the broader political and public interest. I think that's a serious flaw in someone who aspires to be a political leader.'[3]

Howard became leader of the Tory Party and then went on to play a significant part in promoting Cameron as a successor to the post. Howard's judgment is questionable. On the BBC's *Question Time* he would say that if he had been prime minister at the time he would have taken Britain to war anyway, even if he knew that there were no WMD. 'Because Saddam was a threat to peace in the region, and the wider world.' Several lawyers stepped in to point out that what Howard proposed, namely regime change, was illegal under international law.[4]

Lately Howard has prompted banner headlines in the *Daily Mail*: 'Michael Howard is a Tory giant. So how has he got entangled in a slew of doubtful companies – and a fraud probe in a war-torn hell hole?'[5]

It seems that Howard was not content with the sizeable pension due to him as a former leader of Her Majesty's opposition, nor with his £300 per day attendance fee, plus expenses, as a member of the House of Lords, but was looking for a further nest egg to feather his retirement.

Howard secured a part-time post for himself as the Chairman of Soma, a Somalian oil company who were paying him a salary rumoured to be up to £350,000 and also awarding him a seven million share bonus. This could theoretically bring him untold rewards although sadly for Howard and his Get Rich Quick scheme – given the low oil price and the problems caused by a fraud investigation – it now looks unlikely. Furthermore, according to the *Mail*, Howard has been caught up in an investigation by the Serious Fraud Office and although the SFO insists he has done nothing wrong, the investigation is embarrassing to Howard himself and particularly embarrassing to him as one of the big beasts of Brexit. Since a frequent accusation levelled against Brussels by the secessionists is that Europe is a corrupt gravy train, they might be expected to keep their own noses clean.[6]

Cameron's second would-be assassin and Euro-secessionist is Michael Gove. Gove, who believes that the invasion of Iraq was a 'proper British foreign policy success',[7] was perhaps the most unpopular minister of education in the history of that office, gaining a reputation for a high-handed certainty in his own rectitude.

Sarah Caffrey, from Bristol, at the National Union of Teachers' conference in Torquay, has called him an 'evil entity who hovers around and seems to think we're doing such an excellent job we should be working longer and longer hours for less and less pay'.[8]

Interviewed by the children's author Anthony Horovitz for the *Guardian*, Horovitz concluded, 'The truth of the matter is that as our time together slips by, I come to realise that I might as well be interviewing Stonehenge. Everything I throw at him bounces back.'[9]

Gove is presently the justice minister and in the course of his denouncing Cameron, the minister made the mistake of insisting that the terms Cameron had secured for the nation were not enforceable in law and could therefore be regarded only with contempt.

However, unfortunately for Gove, his legal opinion turned out to be false. A former attorney general, Dominic Grieve, pointed out that not only had Cameron's mission to Europe been something of a success, what with Cameron's securing a 'special status' for Britain, but the concessions which Cameron had obtained from the 24 European Heads of State were in fact set in stone. They couldn't be countermanded because they most certainly had legal status.

Thus the ambitious Gove, the Tory minister of justice, was shown to have misunderstood the law in relation to what was now being canvased as one of the most important moments in British history.

Normally if a minister of justice is caught out in ignorance of the law and furthermore if he stubbornly insists that his take on the law is canonical, as Gove has, he might be expected to resign, but not so Gove. Gove is not easily persuaded to fall upon his own sword whatever the reason might be. He is after all a politician with a career and a glorious path to forge.

Famously, ignorance of the law is no defence, least of all in a justice minister – albeit a minister whose concept of justice may leave something to be desired for the egregious Gove has a track record of fiddling his expenses.

Those who are tempted to look to Michael Gove for answers as to how Britain's economy might fare should Brexit succeed might perhaps be aware of Gove's interesting approach to accounting. Gove spent thousands on furnishing his London home before 'flipping' his Commons allowance to a new property in his Surrey constituency, and claiming £13,000 in moving costs. Although he said this was a routine family move he agreed to reimburse Parliament to the tune of £7000.'[10]

Back in his days as a journalist, Gove was once summoned by his employer for a talk about expenses. The boss was curious to know whether Gove had perhaps dated a claim incorrectly, since one of the receipts he'd submitted covered lunch with Kenneth Clarke, the veteran Tory MP. The reason that Gove's boss had found it so curious was because he himself had had lunch with Clarke that same day. Most would consider this awkward, however the slithery Gove, without a pause, simply replied, 'The greedy bastard... two lunches!'[11]

Gove's chutzpah reputedly paid off and he got away with it, but, at the risk of seeming humourless, the first requirement of a minister of justice surely is that he be honest, and that he refrain from lying, however amusingly. The second big beast of Brexit may also be shown to have feet of clay.

Brexit now contains a number of unimpressive also-rans such as the celebrity chef's father, Nigel Lawson, once Margaret Thatcher's economic bagman, and Ian Duncan Smith, the chastiser of those at the bottom of the rung, namely those on benefit. Duncan Smith once described himself as 'the quiet man' in order to create some kind of mystique about himself. The truth was that he had very little to say.

BUT NOW we can come to someone who is widely judged to be the heaviest hitter of all those lining up to wrench the country they claim to love away from the dastardly clutches of a Europe which they see as undermining their sovereignty and hence their own power. They do not want to love their neighbour. They want to divorce him.

Boris Johnson is someone whom the right-wing media are fond of describing as a 'national treasure'. He has a bumbling, blustering and somewhat eccentric manner which some find engaging and others tiresome. He specialises in self-deprecation which some find winning and others calculated.

Johnson has admitted that he employs self-deprecation as a manipulative ploy, to disarm his potential enemies. In an interview with the American TV channel CNBC he declared:

> 'Self-deprecation is a very cunning device... all about understanding that basically people regard politicians as a bunch of shysters, so you've got to be understood... that's what it's all about, I suppose.'[12]

In the light of what lies behind his muddled façade – namely a ruthless and often cruel ambition together with an elitism and a ferocious temper when challenged – it is wrong-headed to describe such a man as a 'national treasure'. Johnson is a man who values himself and his own agenda much more highly than he does the nation or the nation's interest.

His friends say of him approvingly, as if it was a virtue, 'Boris is about Boris.' They're saying this, of course, because they admire the man's remorseless self-promotion and perhaps because, as enthusiastic members of the cult of Boris, they look forward to bathing in his stardust, should he become prime minister for that is surely what he has set his heart on, and what in his madder moments he reveals as his 'destiny' if not his birthright.

When Cameron returned from Europe clutching the new

terms he'd negotiated it was a matter of great public debate as to whether or not Boris Johnson would now loyally support his leader or whether he would jump ship and tie his flag to the 'Britain Must Leave' mast, with all that that would imply.

Johnson heightened the tension by going to ground and refusing to comment either way. His titillation of the media ensured that he made headlines. His house was under siege and eventually he emerged though it was a confused performance. He was clearly wanting it to be seen as a great Churchillian moment. He clearly wished his audience to think, 'look at this wise and heroic figure, this new Pericles, he has to be on the right side of history.'

Instead Johnson's emergence, blinking into the limelight, was something of a damp squib. After much 'excruciating heart-searching' Johnson muttered the usual platitudes about Brussels trumping the British Parliament and then, stopping just short of spelling it out, he made it clear that he was going to be hanging his leader out to dry.

The thirty-year-old rivalry between the two was now out in the open and most observers concluded that Johnson was using Tory divisions over Europe as a pretext for his making a bid for the party leadership. The European issue was to be the trampoline upon which Boris Johnson thought he could bounce his 17-stone self into Number Ten Downing Street.

'Beano Boris', or 'Bonking Boris' as the satirical magazine *Private Eye* (always at a loss as to why anyone should take Johnson seriously) calls him, was making a pitch for the top job.

The prospect was not universally well received. In a Guest Column for the *New Statesman* Boris's former colleague on the *Daily* and *Sunday Telegraph*, Simon Heffer, claimed that 'Even

Boris's senior colleagues dread Tory activists handing him the keys to Downing Street.'

Heffer pointed out that 'it is little wonder that the campaign to leave the European Union was so thrilled to receive Johnson's belated – and confused – endorsement last month. However, he did what the campaign views as the right thing for the wrong reason. When Johnson worked with me in the mid-1990s an Oxford contemporary warned me about him, saying he was the most rampantly ambitious person he had ever met and that he believed in nothing apart from himself.'

Heffer began his column by saying damningly: 'Some people feel that Boris Johnson can do no wrong. They are often those who live vicariously through the celebrities seen on television and followed on the internet, and for whom entertainment is an important distraction. Most entertainment is harmless – no wars have been started or economies wrecked by *I'm a Celebrity…Get Me Out of Here!* or *Strictly Come Dancing*. However, our education in citizenship should extend to understanding that when a politician becomes entertainment first and foremost there is a danger that he, or she, may lack the requisites of statesmanship.'[13]

Shortly after Johnson's announcement that he was backing the Brexit campaign, his long-smouldering antipathy to Cameron was made public in the House of Commons. When Cameron was explaining in detail what it was that he'd achieved in Europe on behalf of his country, Boris could be heard several times boorishly shouting, 'Rubbish!' in quick and emphatic succession, then looking around him in the hope that his fellow MPs would join him in the ribald barracking of his leader.

JOHNSON HAS something about him that feels at home in a braying mob. In his campaign to restore foxhunting (now illegal) and in his preposterously urging fellow-Londoners to take up foxhunting as a way of dealing with urban foxes (Johnson was upset when the Johnson family cat was snapped at by a visiting fox), he's clearly unafraid of the implications of Oscar Wilde's characterising foxhunting as the 'pursuit of the uneatable by the unspeakable' and there are many ways in which Johnson qualifies as unspeakable.

The following quotes should be enough to convey a sense of the mindset of this 'national treasure' whom the governing party in Britain has been turning into a cult figure and crediting with inflated gifts such as his being able to rebrand the Tory Party, so often nicknamed 'the nasty party'.

Unfortunately for such a project Johnson has his own share of nastiness. Johnson believes racism to be 'natural'. Visiting Uganda, Johnson cheerily said to UN workers and their black driver: 'Right, let's go and look at some more piccaninnies'[14] – a racist word previously used by Enoch Powell in his 'rivers of blood' speech against immigration. He likens Chinese workers to 'puffing coolies'.[15] He even favours a return to colonial rule for Africa: 'Left to their own devices,' Johnson has proclaimed, 'the natives would rely on nothing but the instant carbohydrate gratification of the plantain.'[16] 'The problem is not that we were once in charge, but that we are not in charge any more.'[17]

On his watch as editor of the *Spectator* Johnson happily published the Greek playboy 'Taki' with his idle fulminations on 'Bongo-bongo land'[18], on West Indians 'multiplying like flies'[19], on 'black hoodlums' being the root of Britain's social ills and on a 'world Jewish conspiracy' in the course of which Taki describes himself as a '*soi-disant* anti-semite'.[20]

Rather than fire Taki for his arrant racism or even taking him to task, Johnson instead threw a party for him in October 2000 to celebrate Taki's '25 glorious years' as a *Spectator* columnist.

Johnson's sexism doesn't lag far behind: 'The chicks in the *GQ* expenses department – and if you can't call them chicks, then what the hell, I ask you, is the point of writing for *GQ*.' For the benefit of readers of the *Spectator* he claims to have invented the Tottometer – 'the Geiger-counter that detects good-looking women'.[21] Appointing Johnson as editor was in the words of one contributor, like 'entrusting a Ming vase to an ape'.[22]

Johnson has derided renewable energy and he's opposed the Kyoto Treaty on climate change. He supported the homophobic Section 28 and he once compared civil partnerships to 'three men and a dog' getting married.[23] As mayor of London he's scrapped the pledge of the previous mayor, Ken Livingstone, to make 50 per cent of all new homes cheap enough for ordinary London workers – a move which is likely to mean the collapse of buying and renting markets and which will do little to correct the excesses of the London housing market which has seen single properties changing hands for 200 million and which now sees some areas of London in pitch darkness because they are being kept vacant by speculators.

As Denis MacShane has put it, 'As homelessness grows, Europe needs a policy of housing which stops homes being bought as a chip in the casino of modern frontier-free markets but never lived in.'[24]

While the ranks of the homeless in London are burgeoning the super-rich are driving up property prices by seeking out a guaranteed return on their wealth, and they have Boris Johnson to support them.

'We should be humbly thanking the super-rich, not bashing them,' Johnson has declared as he weighs in approvingly on the side of the 'very, very rich', whom he describes as a 'put-upon minority', comparable to the homeless and Irish travellers.

These are the 'zillionaires,' Johnson writes, 'who have other people almost everywhere to do their bidding: people to drive their cars and people to pick up their socks and people to rub their temples with eau de cologne and people to bid for the Munch etching at Christie's.'

Johnson is impressed by such gargantuan wealth and he feels that any resentment of it is misplaced, since in Johnson's view super-rich zillionaires should be offered our 'hearty thanks,' as the top one per cent of earners pay 29.8 per cent of all income tax. According to Johnson, the top one per cent put 'bread on the tables of families who – if the rich didn't invest in supercars and employ eau de cologne-dabbers – might otherwise find themselves without a breadwinner'.

Although, as Bernie Sanders has put it, 'There is something profoundly wrong when the top one-tenth of 1 per cent owns almost as much wealth as the bottom 90 per cent, and when 99 per cent of all new income goes to the top 1 per cent.'

If Johnson believes in anything then he clearly believes in a greed-driven and elitist economy. The idea that each day, capitalism kills far more innocents than died on 9/11, as Dennis Rahkonen has shown, does not even show up on Planet Boris' radar.[25] It's alien to his thought processes. It's irrelevant.

THE IMPLICATION of some of Johnson's other views are equally life-threatening: he has opposed the smoking ban despite improvements in health and atmosphere in pubs and, in much the same way as Ronald Reagan alleged that 'Trees cause more pollution than automobiles do',[26] Johnson has perversely called pedestrians 'the most dangerous features on the roads'[27] and he's vowed to speed up traffic by letting motorbikes use bus lanes. He has adjusted traffic signal timings to give priority to vehicles and less time for pedestrians to cross the road.

'A broad look back at the outgoing mayor's record on road safety shows that the overall number of casualties of all severities has gone up by 5 per cent under Boris Johnson. This is in contrast to the previous mayor Ken Livingstone, who reduced the toll by 38 per cent in eight years. In real numbers that means over 2,500 more people were injured last year than in 2008, the year Boris Johnson became mayor.'[28]

As a motorist reviewing cars for *GQ*, the men's magazine, Johnson presents himself, in the words of his biographer, Sonia Purnell, as 'a sex-obsessed cross between Jeremy Clarkson and Toad of Toad Hall'.

'There is talk,' she notes, 'of blonde drivers 'waggling their rumps,' his own superior horsepower 'taking them from behind,' aided by tantalising thoughts of the imaginary 'ample bosoms' of the female Sat Nav voice.'[29]

Purnell exposes Johnson's desperate desire to display his 'virile superiority' as he describes a Nissan Murano as 'a sort of fat-lipped SUV on steroids' and she quotes from his revealing review: 'Tee-hee!' Johnson coos. 'What was it saying, with the plutocratic sneer of that gleaming grille? It was saying "out of my way, small car driven by ordinary person on modest income. Make way for Murano!"'[30]

More seriously cringe-making was Johnson's support for the Iraq War and the style of it. He was to write in the *Daily Telegraph*: 'That is the best case for Bush; that, among other things, he liberated Iraq. It is good enough for me.'[31] And he would say enthusiastically of the absurd but deadly US President: 'Whenever he appears on TV, I find a cheer rising irresistibly in my throat.'[32]

Yet there is scant consistency in his views. Johnson would make it clear when he was editing the *Spectator*, the influential conservative weekly, that he was giving Bush his full support.

'Not only did I want Bush to win,' Johnson claimed, revealing a lamentable absence of political judgment, 'but we threw the entire weight of the *Spectator* behind him.'[33]

Yet, perversely, in the same year as Johnson claims to be supporting Bush so effusively he writes a *Spectator* leader entitled 'Infantile resentment'.

'The President is a cross-eyed Texan warmonger, unelected, inarticulate, who epitomises the arrogance of American foreign policy.'[34]

This and his other vagaries, which represent something of a political bi-polarity, prompted the *Spectator*'s then owner, Conrad Black, to characterise Johnson as 'ineffably duplicitous'.

Worse however than Johnson's arousing the ire of the soon-to-be discredited jailbird Black, was the fact that he routinely aroused the suspicion and irritation of his fellow journalists. Rory Watson, a Press Association correspondent who worked in Brussels at the same time as Johnson, has claimed that Johnson 'made up stories'. David Usborne of the *Independent* considers Johnson to be 'fundamentally intellectually dishonest in my view. He was serving his masters in a very skilful way but I never felt he believed a word,'[35] and Johnson's Old Etonian contemporary, James Landale, now a senior BBC political editor, went into verse about Boris the journalist's lies after his having experienced them at first hand in Brussels:

Boris told such dreadful lies
It made one gasp and stretch one's eyes.

Johnson had arrived in Brussels to work for the *Daily Telegraph* having just been fired by the *Times* for inventing quotations and for attributing them to an Oxford professor at Balliol, Dr. Colin Lucas, who, since he was Boris Johnson's own godfather, had no reason to mistrust Boris, his journalist godson. Lucas' trust proved entirely misplaced.

Lucas was an archaeologist who had discovered the remains of Edward II's 14th-century 'Rosary' Palace in Hay's Wharf, south London. To spice up his story, Johnson saw fit to fabricate a comment from his godfather about the monarch's sexual exploits with his favourite, Piers Gaveston. Johnson falsely quoted Professor Lucas as saying the king 'had enjoyed a reign of dissolution with his catamite, Piers Gaveston' in the palace.

Unfortunately for Johnson the palace was built in 1325 and Gaveston had been beheaded in 1312 and Johnson had never, in fact, bothered to discuss the subject in any detail with his godfather. Fearful of the damage to his academic reputation, an angry, betrayed and humiliated Lucas got in touch with the *Times* and complained. According to Andrew Gilmour, who was at Balliol with both Lucas and Johnson, 'Lucas was a laughing stock. Every sub-lecturer from Sheffield wrote in to point out his error.'[36]

When quizzed by the *Times'* editor, Charlie Wilson, Johnson made the mistake of digging the hole he was in more deeply. He insisted that he'd spoken to Lucas and that he'd got the erroneous information from him. But of course he hadn't. He was lying. Misled by Johnson, the editor of the *Times* wrote to Lucas saying, 'Our reporter stands by his story.' The hurt and angry Lucas complained again.

The *Times* now took Johnson's breach of their journalistic code seriously: for attributing his own historical mistake to that of a distinguished archaeologist and historian; for sexing up the story at Lucas' expense, and for lying to the *Times* about having spoken to Lucas to obtain the quote when he hadn't done so, Johnson was fired.

The Parliamentary sketch-writer Simon Hoggart wittily commented that it was all 'amazing, since it means that yesterday Piers Gaveston had brought a national leader to his knees for the first time in 700 years'.[37]

Challenged about this later Johnson attempted to play it down by saying that he'd just 'mildly sandpapered something someone said'.[38]

And even now he continues to blame 'fact-grubbing historians' for his *Times* downfall.[39]

Given such a past, it might be thought that on arriving in Brussels to work for the *Telegraph* Johnson would pay more attention to the truth, but the reverse proved to be the case.

The first story Johnson filed concerned the Berlaymont building in Brussels, the headquarters of the European Commission. During the building's refurbishment it had to be evacuated due to an asbestos problem. In Johnson's hands, however, the story is re-jigged in order to titillate the Europhobia of the *Daily Telegraph*'s owners and readers. The building, a symbol of European governance, was, Johnson claimed, to be 'blown up'. But it wasn't. The news story that Johnson had filed was quite untrue.

Shortly afterwards he followed this story up with a story for the *Sunday Telegraph*, 'Delors Plan to Rule Europe'. Again this was perhaps more influenced by some projection of Johnson's own childhood – his toddler ambition to be 'the World King' and later to be president of the United States[40] (he was born in New York and until recently held a US passport) – rather than by any salient facts.

Johnson wrote that it had been 'reported that Delors wanted to scrap the rotation of the EU presidency and to centralise power in Brussels. The member states would lose their remaining veto rights.'[41]

But it wasn't true. It was pure invention. However there was a sub-text: the popular British tabloids had begun to specialise in shock-horror stories about the EU. They were deliberately designed to create fears about Europe and they were invariably untrue.

In September 1994, for example, all of the British tabloids insisted that Brussels was going to ban curved or small bananas. Only straight bananas were to be sold. This was untrue.

On 21 February 2005 the *Sun* claimed that 'EU health chiefs are drawing up plans to close thousands of British off-licences.' It was untrue.

Here is the *Daily Star* on the same date: 'Supermarkets will only be able to sell booze at weekends under secret plans by barmy Brussels bureaucrats.' Again untrue.

Not to be outdone, in October 1997 the *Daily Mail* claimed that the EU was 'about to abolish the British loaf. Brussels bureaucrats are planning the end of the British standard loaf.' Untrue, as a visit to any supermarket would reveal.

In his book on Brexit the former Labour MP Denis Mac-Shane suggested that 'it would take a whole book to list all the myths and half-truths about Europe.'

Interestingly, MacShane goes on 'to trace a starting point' and he singles out Boris Johnson as being the man who 'invented Eurosceptic news reporting.' According to MacShane,

'The arrival of Boris Johnson as the Brussels correspondent of the *Daily Telegraph* in 1989, a year after Mrs Thatcher's Bruges speech, was the moment when telling lies about Europe became official British newspaper policy. The *Daily Telegraph* was also in foreign ownership and was on the eve of becoming the cheerleader for crude anti-European ideology.'[42]

Here is an example of its crudity, in a typical Boris Johnson *canard:*

> First they make us pay in our taxes for Greek olive groves, many of which probably don't exist. Then they say we can't dip our bread in olive oil in restaurants. We didn't join the Common Market – betraying the New Zealanders and their butter – in order to be told when, where and how we must eat the olive oil we have been forced to subsidise.[43]

Another fabrication, of course, and the trend pioneered by him continues. A recent headline proclaimed, 'Europe steals our coastline' but instead of any vampire-like Europe being responsible for the coastal erosion of its neighbouring British islands the story would turn out merely to be concerned with the EU trying to coordinate coastguards in order to improve its response to refugees at sea.

ONE OF THE CHARGES made against the European Union by the secessionists, the 'little Englanders', is that it is undemocratic (although they forget the fact that they have MEP's, Members of the European Parliament, whom they can vote in and out.)

In their arguments against Britain remaining in the Union they refer, with ill-concealed patriotism, to their own Parliament as being the living exemplar of democracy, the mother of Parliaments, no less, and hence, they say, it would quite wrong for them to devolve one iota of that Parliament's sovereignty to the undemocratic and demonised Brussels.

By a comic irony however a closer look at the British Parliament reveals a highly undemocratic institution housed within the Palace of Westminster. As if in some feudal stately home, some 5000 servants work within the building, bowing and scraping in its heavily subsidised restaurants and bars and offices to a group of state officials in the House of Commons and in the House of Lords – the largest proportion of the latter being entirely unelected.

There is, in fact, a preponderance of legislators within the building who have absolutely no democratic mandate whatsoever. There are, for example, twenty-six Bishops, representatives of the state religion, the Church of England. The House of Lords is also stacked to the rafters with party donors – a million pounds or two will secure a peerage.

Since the baronetcy – a quaint hereditary knighthood – was devised by King James in the early 17th century specifically to raise cash, honours have been for sale. Subtly so, but unquestionably for sale. When Salisbury became prime minister for the first time in 1885, he said that dealing with those who aspired to become lords or knights had 'been a revelation to me of the baser side of human nature'. 'People are rather apt,' echoed Curzon, 'supposing they see in the newspapers that an honour has been conferred upon some person unknown to themselves, to imagine that the honour has been bought.' People's aptitude for sensing mephitic stenches hovering around the honours system is correct. The chain-store grocer, David Sainsbury, gives two million to the Labour Party on long loan and then, *mirabile dictu*, he becomes Lord Sainsbury. There are other examples too numerous to mention.

With its 792 members, the House of Lords overflowing with its tuft-hunters – its dubiously ennobled and favoured appointees – is the only second chamber in the world which is larger than its Parliament's first chamber: the elected House of Commons has just 650 members. The mother of Parliaments is thus intrinsically undemocratic and even invites comparison with Iran, it being the only other State legislature which includes representatives of its state religion, as of right.

Here is Johnson on the allegations of gravy-train politics in the EU: 'With every year of its existence, the Euro-parliament deepens the general suspicion of the public – that the EU is a racket, and that the MEPs are on a gigantic boondoggle.'[44]

At the same time as Johnson wrote this, however, he was earning £250,000 p. a. from writing articles in this vein for the *Daily Telegraph* (a hefty sum that he'd grandiosely dismiss as 'chicken feed' on the BBC's programme *Hardtalk* and which would later rise to £500,000) and for several years Johnson would also be combining this with his mayoral salary of £150,000, along with his MP's salary and expenses. Since his own snout was so very firmly in the trough he could hardly make allegations about EU gravy-train politics and he was most certainly in no position to do so when his own employment policy at the Eurosceptic *Spectator* would reek of nepotistic corruption.

So keen was Johnson on allowing the *Spectator* to serve his own ends that at one point it came to be nicknamed the *Johnsonator*. Johnson used it, for example, to give frequent employment to his brother Leo, to his sister Rachel, and to her husband Ivo Dawnay. His father Stanley was hired to write on the environment, and his father-in-law Charles Wheeler was engaged to write on foreign affairs.[45]

The Johnson dynasty's lust for self-promotion is notorious. The paterfamilias of the Johnson brood, Stanley Johnson, 'never ceases to trumpet their achievements, even ostentatiously counting the number of times his family appears in one day's newspapers in the public arena of his local newsagent'.[46]

In Johnson's first year in office as mayor of London he personally spent £4,698 on taxis. One journey alone cost the taxpayer £237, prompting a witty blogger to comment: 'Where exactly does Boris cycle? Is it just to and from photo-shoots?'[47]

Johnson's riding a bicycle around town can, of course, have as much to do with his projecting Brand Boris as it does with any serious environmental concerns. Johnson keeps two cars after all in his £2.3 million Georgian townhouse overlooking Regent's Canal and he's a climate change denier, but a bicycle can look good and it enables him to feel superior.

On one occasion Johnson made a great show of pitting his bicycle against what he thought was a ministerial car in which the Labour MP Keith Vaz was travelling. According to Johnson, as the vehicle passed him on a street in Whitehall, 'Vaz hauled down the window to hail me. Actually, I can't be sure that it was Vaz who pressed the button. It might have been him, or the driver, or the bodyguard.' Keith Vaz then offered Johnson a lift. However, in an article in the *Daily Telegraph* entitled 'LIMO-LOVING POLITICIANS' Johnson would describe the lift as having been offered 'in the kindly tones of Louis XIV leaning from his carriage to comfort a poor peasant woman struggling along in the mud'. Johnson refuses. '"No, it's OK, thanks, Keith," I said, slapping the battered old handlebars of my machine, "I've got my bike."'

Johnson then decried the cost to the taxpayer of Vaz's 'grandiose entourage'. Here was Vaz, Johnson added, 'cruising around London as though he was Charles blooming de Gaulle'. For good measure he castigated Vaz's 'rear end' as the 'symbol of everything wrong with British politics' – it being, Johnson claimed, 'cupped, cosseted, cocooned on the velour upholstery of a government car'.

The only problem with Johnson's story was that Vaz's behind was in fact firmly planted on the seat of the Vaz family's Prius for, as a mere select committee chairman, Vaz was not entitled to a ministerial car let alone to have a chauffeur or a bodyguard. The car was in fact being driven by Vaz's assistant and the fantasy was, in Vaz's words, 'all a nonsense'.[48]

Johnson had twisted a non-event to his own ends and had maliciously put Keith Vaz in a bad light simply in order to earn his quarter to half a million pound salary from the *Daily Telegraph*.[49]

Johnson's distortion of the facts to suit himself was evident at Oxford if not before. When he was an undergraduate, Johnson had fervently wished to become president of the Oxford Union, widely considered a stepping-stone to political success in the outside world. This was a post for which the Union rulebook forbade outright canvasing. However Johnson cavalierly ignored Union procedure and canvased vigorously on his own behalf:

> On one occasion he even handed out bottles of red wine to Gridiron members in a particularly brazen, even crass attempts to 'buy' their votes. 'Such displays of naked ambition were totally out of place,' recalls one undergraduate there that day.[50]

On another occasion Johnson tried to bamboozle his way into the presidential office by deception. Judging *en route* that the Conservative Party was less popular amongst Oxford's student

body than in the Tory shires he told Union members – his potential voters – that he was a member of the SDP, the Social
Democratic Party. He was not.

To his chagrin he was unelected. His state-school rival,
Neil Sherlock, who had a broader appeal was returned with
a sizeable majority despite Johnson having got his glamorous
girlfriend, Allegra Mostyn-Owen, to try and persuade Sherlock
behind the scenes, 'not to stand against "my Boris"'.[51]

Sonia Purnell describes how 'a good deal of snobbish and
unpleasant personal abuse was heaped on Sherlock by Boris
supporters, who pulled faces and called him a "horrible, spermy
little man", who spoke with a "funny accent" and who was
"patently uncharismatic"'.[52]

In the run-up to the election as London mayor Johnson
would adopt a similar ploy to that which he employed at the
Oxford Union for his London hustings. At a meeting of the
London Citizens' Convention in Westminster's Methodist
Central Hall Johnson described himself as 'the grandson of a
Muslim immigrant from Turkey'. He fondly hoped this would
counteract all the 'racist' chatter about him but since his self-
description was inaccurate, it didn't.[53]

On Johnson's second try at being elected to the Oxford
Union he was successful and he would explain his subsequent
success in an essay called 'Politics'. What you needed, according to Johnson, was 'a disciplined and deluded collection of
stooges' to get the vote out for you in their respective colleges.

As Andrew Gimson, Johnson's first biographer, points out,
'The key word here is "deluded"'. Johnson's stooges were
recruited by his trick of intimating that he'd do something for
them once elected even if he had every intention of forgetting
all about them. Johnson reveals his cynically manipulative tech-

nique: 'The relationship... is founded on duplicity.' Johnson goes on: 'The tragedy of the stooge is that even if he thinks this through, he wants so much to believe that his relationship with the candidate is special that he shuts out the truth. The terrible art of the candidate is to coddle the self-deception of the stooge.'[54]

Gimson judges Johnson's analysis of how to become president of the Oxford Union as 'worthy of Machiavelli'.[55]

Such behaviour didn't make him popular. Lloyd Evans, the editor of the Oxford University satirical magazine *Tributary* noted that during the build-up to the Union presidency election 'he [Johnson] became fixated about what we were writing about him.'

They were preparing an issue which 'contained a whole stream of abuse of Boris. We called him an exiled Armenian chicken farmer. The other thing we called him was the Aryan bull pig, victim of a hideous Nazi war experiment in 1936. We'd also call him incompetent. That was the thing he picked up on [...] He was absolutely incandescent. He really went mad. He grabbed the typewriter and said, 'Damn it, I'm a journalist,' and started writing his own version of the whole thing. We ended up not publishing any of it. I was surprised by how angry he was.'[56] Elsewhere Evans is quoted as saying that Johnson's anger 'was coming from a deep, dark place'.[57]

Ever unpredictable, opportunistic and volatile Johnson rivals Donald Trump, to whom he bears a certain similarity in a shameless ability to contradict himself and yet to believe that he's right on each occasion, and also in his belief that he has a licence to lie, particularly if he can come up with a vivid enough excuse to mask his deception.

The master in College at Eton, Martin Hammond, would

say of him, 'Boris sometimes seems affronted when criticised [...] I think he honestly believes that it is churlish of us not to regard him as an exception.'[58]

Famously Johnson would characterise reports he had cheated on his wife with a colleague at the *Spectator*, Petronella Wyatt, as 'an inverted pyramid of piffle'. This oddly phrased denial was to no avail however when the affair was confirmed by Petronella Wyatt's mother, and when various friends of Wyatt inconveniently briefed newspapers that she'd had two abortions and that she'd understandably felt betrayed by the then Tory arts spokesman.[59]

Johnson's instinctive dishonesty was clear from their relationship. 'Faced with one of Petronella's pregnancies, he said she should have an affair with someone and say it was their child.'[60]

His dishonesty colours another relationship with one Helen MacIntyre whom Johnson appointed as his Arts adviser when he was mayor. Johnson has had a child with MacIntyre but, despite the glaring evidence of the child's albino-cum-blond hair of its father, Johnson insists that the child's hair is 'ginger'.[61] It isn't.

Unfortunately for Johnson his dishonesty proved too much for Michael Howard, his then Party leader (and now his Brexit comrade-in-arms), and Howard was to sack him from his junior Cabinet post for lying about the Wyatt affair.

While Boris Johnson's fans like to describe him as 'political Viagra', he can be described less attractively but with equal accuracy as a louche bully to whom lying comes as second nature and with a distinctly unpleasant fascination with violence.

In a *Vanity Fair* profile, the writer Michael Wolff tailed Johnson for a day or two and listened to his speeches. He commented, 'It's all riff – anti-political correctness, anti-personal regulation, pro the verities of English life (hunting and smoking and smacking).'[62]

Depending on your point of view Johnson's beloved English 'verities' can equally be described as animal torture, self-harm and child abuse.

Johnson is pro-hunting and in promoting the cause he reveals how he has benefited gastronomically from stag hunting on Exmoor where his father, Stanley Johnson, owns some 500 acres. The stag in question was surrounded by the hounds in the middle of the river Exe. 'I can see it now,' Johnson recalls, 'stepping high in the water, eyes rolling, tongue protruding, foaming, antlers streaming bracken and leaves like the hat of some demented old woman, and behind is the sexual, high-pitched yipping of the dogs [...] I can remember the ventral cavity. Then they cut out the heart and gave it to my six-year-old brother, still beating, he claimed ever afterwards, or still twitching, and he went dancing home singing: 'We've got the heart! We've got the heart!' So we cooked it up with a bit of flour, and the German *au pair* girl left the next day.'
Johnson describes his exhilaration at demonstrating in favour of hunting together with 80,000 hearty members of the Countryside Alliance and concludes that 'hunting is best for the deer.'[63]

During a celebrity England-Germany game of football, Johnson is caught on film making a twenty-yard charge designed to floor a German player by sinking his head into the player's stomach – a possessed move which, had he been a professional player, would have led to his being sent off the pitch or worse. The film footage records a rugby tackle in a game of soccer of a gratuitous and almost deranged violence.

Johnson's propensity for violence goes back to his school-days. His school newspaper, the *Eton Chronicle*, echoed the anti-Vietnam war chant when noting the violence which Alexander Boris Johnson employed while playing the Eton Wall Game: 'Hey! Hey! ABJ! How many Oppidans did you kill today?'[64]

Johnson was, according to his biographer, Andrew Gimson, 'intensely proud of his achievements at school and loved being a leader there'.

The Eton College tradition was that when you left the school you'd make an entry in the College Leaving Book. There was room for a comment and a Leaver Portrait of your-self taken by an approved school photographer.

On Johnson's departure the College Leaving Book was found to contain 'a large photograph of himself, with two scarves and a machine gun, together with an inscription about his determi-nation to achieve "more notches on my phallocratic phallus"'.[65]

JOHNSON'S PENCHANT for an almost sexualised violence would soon find a further outlet in the initiation rites of Oxford's Bullingdon Club. Johnson was proud to be a member of the two-hundred-year-old dining and drinking club and would stand for its presidency. He was a keen participant in its excesses – raucous rituals described by an ex-member in the *Guardian*: 'There's the air of lurking violence, and above all the sense that its members consider themselves above the law on such occasions.'[66]

The club, whose youthful members like to dress up as if they belonged to a high powered and gold-braided military elite, once enjoyed a 'famously explosive dinner' at the White Hart near Oxford in 2005: 'All the food and plates had been thrown everywhere and they were jumping on top of each other on the table like kids in a playground,' recalled the pub's landlord Ian Rogers. The part he found strangest was that each time he confronted a member of the club 'they apologised profusely but offered absolutely no explanation.'[67]

The Bullingdon Club is for plutocratic undergraduates who think nothing of spending £3,500 on its royal blue tailcoats with ivory lapels and canary yellow waistcoats – a livery which prompted Evelyn Waugh in *Brideshead Revisited* to describe the Bullingdon members as looking like a bunch of 'very disorderly footmen'[68] and as 'baying for broken glass'.[69]

The Bullingdon is still banned from meeting within a 15-mile radius of Christ Church after the time in 1927 when they smashed over 400 windows in the college's Peckwater Quadrangle. In Waugh's novel *Decline and Fall* published the following year, the Bullingdon appears as the 'Bollinger' whose annual dinner was accompanied by 'a confused roaring and a breaking of glass'.

'It is not accurate,' Waugh says, in a description that is now almost a hundred years old but which still applies, 'to call this an annual event, because quite often the club is suspended for some years after each meeting.'

There is tradition behind the Bollinger; it numbers reigning kings among its past members. At the last dinner, three years ago, a fox had been brought in in a cage and stoned to death with champagne bottles. What an evening that had been! This was the first meeting since then, and from all over Europe old members had rallied for the occasion. For two days they had been pouring into Oxford: epileptic royalty from their villas of exile; uncouth peers from crumbling country seats; smooth young men of uncertain tastes from embassies and legations; illiterate lairds from wet granite hovels in the Highlands;

ambitious young barristers and Conservative candidates torn from the London season and the indelicate advances of debutantes; all that was most sonorous of name and title was there for the beano.

The current minister of foreign affairs in Poland, Radek Sikorski, formerly of Pembroke College was surprised to be woken up in the middle of the night in his lodgings in Oxford's Walton Street and to be met by the sight of a marauding mob led by Boris Johnson, all whooping and chortling as Sikorski's room was trashed and his possessions destroyed by cricket bats and cricket stumps wielded with sadistic glee.

Sikorski sat up in his bed, bemused. 'In the middle of the night,' Sikorski recalls, 'a dozen screaming figures burst into my room and demolished it completely.'[70]

This was the Bullingdon Club's thuggish way of telling someone that they'd just been made a member and that, having endured this introductory ritual without complaint, they would now be privileged to do the same thing to new members and to enjoy themselves in similar fashion at their expense: to shred their clothes; to rip their books in half; to hurl their hi-fi systems to the ground while wine bottles were emptied onto a pile of their belongings in the centre of the room and while photographs of girl friends were ripped up and decried.

In a piece penned by Barney Ronay in the *Guardian* called 'Young, rich and drunk', Ronay writes:

Then there's the Bullingdon's committed and longstanding misogyny. It's not just the all-male exclusivity, more the tales of hiring strippers to preside at the initiation of new members at the annual breakfast. Plus the trapped, frantic and vaguely sexual energy of the whole thing. The Bullingdon is simply a no-go area for women. These are teenagers almost exclusively from an all-male boarding school background. It's no real surprise that some of the naive, hostile and retarded attitudes fostered there resurface at a university reunion. You just have to hope they grow out of it.[71]

Another stock-in-trade of the Bullingdon initiation rituals was for newly elected members to visit Bonn Square where Oxford's homeless congregate and to burn £50 notes in front of them by way of jeering at their misfortune.[72]

The Club is most noteworthy for its trashing of the restaurants which it's booked for its antics and then for its members to assume that they could exonerate themselves by throwing banknotes at the hapless, and possibly ruined, proprietors.

Hilaire Belloc had it in his *Cautionary Tales*:

Like many of the Upper Class
He liked the sound of broken glass.

Belloc could well have been thinking of the members of the Bullingdon Club. At one club meal in 1987, attended by both Johnson and Cameron, someone (whose identity has never been properly established due to the Bullingdon rule of *omertà)* threw a large plant pot through the restaurant window.

The burglar alarm was activated and the Oxford police duly descended on the dining club's chosen venue with their sniffer dogs. Six of the group were apprehended and spent the night at Cowley police station.

Cameron escaped but Johnson's attempt to evade the police by running off and crawling through a hedge in the Botanical Gardens failed and, by his own account, an overnight stay in a police cell reduced him to 'a gibbering namby-pamby'– proving the truth of the age-old adage that a bully caught out usually proves a coward.

Cameron seems sheepish about his Bullingdon past. When asked by the TV interviewer Andrew Marr whether he was embarrassed about it the Tory leader replied: 'Of course, desperately, very embarrassed about it.' Johnson, however, seems proud of his Bullingdon membership and reputedly relishes hailing former members of the Club, so distinguished for its destructive binges, with a braying chant of 'Buller! Buller! Buller!' which he expects to be reciprocated in a tribal bonding ritual.

His defence of privilege is a persistent theme. In 1980, after extolling the virtues of private education he concluded, 'So strain every nerve, parents of Britain, to send your son to this educational establishment (forget this socialist gibberish about the destruction of the State System). Exercise your freedom of choice because in this way you imbue your son with the most important thing, a sense of his own importance.'[73]

The unfairness of the public schools' leech-like presence within the country's education system and their unwarranted charitable status doesn't faze Johnson for a moment.

He admires and he serves economic elitism. Eighty per cent of those who backed his campaign for the office of mayor of London were from the financial sector – from hedge-funders, from private equity experts, from financial service houses and from multi-millionaire businessmen – something that may have weighed with Johnson's later attacking the top tax rate for high earners and with his regarding 'banker bashers' as deluded.

In November 2013 Johnson would go as far as describing the super-wealthy as 'a put upon minority' and he ludicrously described them as being 'like Irish travellers and the homeless'. In that same year the super-wealthy would bag an average 14% pay rise while the average wage rose by a paltry below inflation 0.7%.

Sonia Purnell has pointed out, 'since his first months in office, Boris's attitude towards the City and the super-rich has been at odds with his 'Mayor of the People' persona. As Simon Jenkins of the *Standard* tellingly puts it: 'His defence of bankers' greed is Bullingdon morality, pure and simple.'[74]

Johnson's more sensitive sister Rachel, a novelist, has commented on an infamous Bullingdon Club photograph that features both her brother and Cameron: 'It looks what it is, elitist, arrogant, privileged and of an age that would have little resonance with people on low incomes who didn't go to Eton.'[75]

In the 'overbearing arrogance embodied in these sub-Gainsborough postures – in the twittish clothing, the floppy hair and the almost luminous sense of false entitlement which radiate from these historic images'[76] – it's not hard to hazard a guess at their subsequent career paths.

IN ADDITION TO Johnson and Cameron, the photograph also features a close friend of Boris Johnson's, one Darius Guppy – a man who shortly after leaving University was to embark upon a criminal career, and a man who is also widely suspected to have led Johnson himself – given Johnson's toleration of violence – into criminality.

As Johnson's first biographer, Andrew Gimson, has put it, 'No scandal, or alleged scandal, has pursued Boris for longer than the bizarre case of his tape recorded conversation with his Eton and Oxford chum Darius Guppy.'[77]

Darius Guppy was aggrieved that his father, a partner in the Lloyds insurance partnership, had lost much of his fortune together with the family home through a Lloyds implosion in 1989 in which massive claims being made against some Lloyds partners arrived all at once – most of them for the environmental damage caused by asbestos and by the Exxon Valdes oil spill.

Guppy felt that, in his words, 'certain Lloyds agents were in large measure responsible for what had happened, putting investors' money into dicey syndicates that would one day collapse under massive insurance claims.'

Non-business folk such as Guppy's father were wilfully 'lured into Lloyds through a massive recruitment campaign, and while an avalanche of claims were hanging over the market'.[78]

By way of revenge against the company he held liable for his family's misfortune, Guppy planned an elaborate insurance fraud. In March 1990 Guppy arranged to have himself and his business partner, Ben Marsh, tied up in a room in the Halloran House Hotel in New York – the world's largest gem centre – and to make it appear as if they'd been robbed of jewels worth £1.8 million.

Guppy recruited an Englishman called Peter Risdon to play the part of the robber. They'd met Risdon in London while he was working for Counter Spy, purveyors of surveillance equipment in South Audley Street in Mayfair and where Risdon had boasted to them of his alleged criminal activities.

They required him to tie them both up and, for good measure, to fire a bullet into Guppy's pillow. Guppy and Marsh were then to make a successful claim against Lloyd's from which, having convinced Lloyd's loss adjustors that their losses were genuine, they were to profit handsomely to the tune of £1.8 million.

The New York police however were suspicious and when they questioned them both about the identity of the robber (whom Guppy and Marsh had falsely identified as being American), the NYPD investigating officer, detective Raymond Berke from the 17th Precinct, was alerted by the robber's allegedly asking both Guppy and Marsh to 'lie down on your front.'

The normal American expression would have been 'Lie face down.' 'Lie down on your front' was, the NYPD detective judged, what an Englishman would say.

There were other inconsistencies to do with angle of the firing of the gun and its residual powder-marks which prompted the NYPD officer to wonder if this wasn't a sting – staged by three Englishmen. He passed the details onto Scotland Yard.

As it happened Peter Risdon, the 'robber', had also had been having his own suspicions about Guppy. Risdon believed that he was going to be framed for the crime and the chances were that, instead of his sharing in the proceeds, that he'd be languishing in a US jail while Guppy and Marsh, having cheated him, would escape to South America with their very considerable rewards. Risdon therefore took the precaution of tapping into Guppy's telephone and recording his conversations.

At around the same time a *News of the World* journalist, Stuart Collier, had been making some inquiries about Guppy and, to his consternation, Guppy had discovered that Collier, in the course of his writing a profile of him for his paper, had been passing some information about Guppy to the New York police.

For the time being Guppy and Marsh, now back in England, have got away with it. Lloyds have compensated them for the jewelry and understandably they wish to continue getting away with it and so Guppy, now back in England, promptly turns to his old friend, Boris Johnson, a fellow Old Etonian and former Bullingdon Club member, for help.

Guppy is determined to put Collier off the scent and he's

decided that the best way to do this is by employing scare tactics. He informs Johnson that he's either going to beat Collier up himself or that he'll 'hire some heavies to do it'. He asks Johnson to find out Collier's address.

Instead of discouraging his friend from this course of action Johnson appears to indulge Guppy's violent and criminal proclivities. Unfortunately for both Guppy and Johnson, Risdon the 'robber' was recording the 21-minute call in which Johnson can be heard discussing how badly the journalist will be beaten up and agreeing to use his journalistic contacts in order to be able to supply Guppy with Stuart Collier's address and telephone number – the journalist who is threatening to expose Guppy and Marsh's fraudulent scam.

It is clear from what passes between Guppy and Johnson that this isn't the only conversation that they've had about the subject. Johnson is at pains to appear compliant saying, 'I got this bloody number for you. OK, Darry. I said I'd do it. I'll do it', and that Guppy knows Johnson has been obliging him by putting out feelers amongst his newspaper contacts – four of whom have already indicated to Johnson that they will come back to Johnson with Collier's details.[79]

Johnson must be familiar enough with English law to know that if anything happened to Collier and, if Johnson's part in it were to be discovered, then these exchanges would make him what in common law is known as an 'accessory before the fact'. In other words, it would make him criminally liable.

Consequently Johnson is at pains to impress upon Guppy how crucial it is that his, Johnson's, complicity be concealed. Guppy assures Johnson that his part in what both parties must assuredly know to be a crime will be untraceable to Johnson. Johnson then seems less apprehensive and promises to provide

Guppy with the prospective victim's address. Johnson's exact and incriminating words to Guppy on tape are: 'I got this bloody number for you. OK Darry, I said I'll do it and I'll do it. Don't worry.'

Once Guppy has been provided with the address he flies from Cape Town to London. Accounts now vary as to what exactly happened. Stuart Collier is apparently no longer a journalist and has gone to ground but, according to Guppy himself, Guppy lay in wait for Collier, knocked the hapless journalist to the ground and covered him in manure. In other accounts, Collier is set upon and badly beaten.

It seems too that while Collier's offence in Guppy's eyes was his threatening to expose Guppy and Marsh's insurance fraud he was also threatening to cast aspersions on Guppy's wife's past.

He angrily explains to Johnson that he wishes to avenge himself on a 'tabloid scuzzbag' who has reduced his wife to tears. Collier, in Guppy's eyes, is doubly deserving of a serious bruising if not indeed a few broken bones. Guppy emphasises that it is 'no worse than what happened to you in Rugby'. Johnson does not at any point demur, nor does this Tory advocate of law and order take exception to the idea of two old friends conspiring to take the law into their own hands, even though blood seems likely to be shed.

The taped conversation was recorded at Guppy's then home in Chelsea in the summer of 1990. At the time of the phone call, Johnson was working for the *Daily Telegraph* in Brussels. Here is an excerpt from the transcript:

JOHNSON: If it got out ...

GUPPY interrupts: That he'd been beaten up.

JOHNSON: Beaten up, it would inevitably get back to the contact.

Johnson then says that he has used four contacts to track down information about Collier, but that he's worried one of them 'might put two and two together, if he heard that this guy [Collier] had been beaten up…'

GUPPY interrupts him: But Boris there's absolutely no ******* proof: you just deny it. I mean, there's no proof at all…

JOHNSON: Well yeah.

GUPPY: I mean, you know, big deal. You're sitting in Brussels and the day it happens you're in Brussels, it's as simple as that.

Guppy repeatedly appeals to Johnson to have faith in him. At one stage Johnson replies in a slightly slavish tone, 'I do have faith in you.'

GUPPY continues: As far as I'm concerned, I have never told you what I require this number for. You do not know at all … so you are totally off the hook.' He adds: 'You have nothing to fear. I give you my personal guarantee, OK, and my word of honour.

By the end of the conversation, Johnson says that he has the requested details and that he will divulge them. He is volunteering to do what he can to help even though Guppy has spelled out the negative ways in what way Johnson's help will affect Collier's wellbeing. Guppy says: 'He will probably get a couple of black eyes and a… a cracked rib or something.'

Johnson expresses no real concern at all about the man's probable injuries. His sole concern is for his own back.

Guppy repeatedly reassures him:

We'll do it discreetly. That's all I require – just the address: the address and the phone number ... all right? Now I guarantee

you, you have nothing to worry about. *[Slowly, emphatically]* Believe me. All right? You have my personal guarantee. I've never let you down, all right?

JOHNSON: I got this bloody number for you. OK Darry, I said I'll do it and I'll do it. Don't worry.[80]

The reason for Peter Risdon's going public with the tape was that he had found himself increasingly disillusioned by the duplicity of modern politicians and that he'd decided that this, at least, would be one way of catching one meretricious MP in the act.

When in April 2009, to Johnson's obvious discomfort, excerpts from Risdon's tape were aired for the first time as part of a *Dispatches* TV programme called 'The Trouble With Boris', Johnson squirmed and swallowed hard and then attempted to brush it off by saying: 'It was all a bit of a joke. It was all rather harmless. It was just Darry [Guppy's nickname].'[81]

When confronted by the film-maker Michael Cockerell with more extensive extracts from the recording for a BBC programme, *The Irresistible Rise of Boris Johnson*, Johnson again tried to laugh it off, but could be seen to be shifting his physical position in obvious anguish. He claimed that the sound-clips 'were taken out of context' and he insisted twice that 'nothing eventuated from that conversation.'[82] But the latter was not true.

Asked how he felt while listening to the recording Johnson briskly snapped that it was 'a load of old cobblers' but of course it wasn't. The recording was authentic and while Johnson was claiming on camera that 'nothing eventuated' from the call,

Guppy himself was, and is, in no doubt about what he did to Collier once he'd been supplied with his whereabouts by Johnson.

In an interview which Guppy gave to the *Daily Mail* on his release from prison, Guppy boasted, 'I knocked him [Stuart Collier] to the ground and tipped slurry on his head'.[83]

The *Daily Mail* made it clearer still:

Boris Johnson's friend Guppy, 49, says he flew from Cape Town to London to exact revenge on the man. He took exception to an article he believed 'humiliated' his wife, Patricia. Guppy is an old friend of the Mayor of London and of Earl Spencer. In 1993 he was jailed for organising a faked jewellery heist for £1.8m insurance.[84]

Elsewhere Guppy speaks of giving a tabloid journalist 'the hiding which most of us secretly admit such people deserve'. Asked if he has any regrets, Guppy responds, 'Only that I was never able to finish the job.'[85]

Later in an article in the *New Statesman* Guppy would confirm in greater detail that, despite Johnson's denials that anything had happened and despite his alternative claim that it was 'all a joke' he, Guppy, had most assuredly attacked Collier:

Having discovered his [Collier's] address and flown into London from South Africa where I live, I waited for him to emerge from his house, chased him, and then, having knocked him to the ground, emptied over his head a sack of horse manure rendered slurry by the addition of bottled water – a concoction made possible courtesy of Hyde Park Riding School and the springs of Évian.

The aim had been not to hurt him but to humiliate him as he had sought to humiliate my wife. And humiliate him is exactly what I did, in front of his neighbours who had poured out on to the street at the sound of his screams.

Guppy claims he also had two 'accomplices, who did not touch him', whom he said had recorded the event, but did not upload it onto the internet.[86]

Confronted again by the details of this affair while he was running for the office of mayor of London, Boris Johnson made a slightly different attempt to brush it off by saying of his old friend that he lived by 'the Homeric code of honour, loyalty and revenge'. But his attempt to dignify what was a squalid and brutal chain of events by bamboozling his interlocutor with rarefied classical references was an obvious ploy.

He and Guppy were not Hector and Achilles in some new Trojan War fighting the forces of darkness. Instead Guppy was a fraudster soon to be jailed for five years for staging a fake jewellery heist in an insurance scam and, as the tape recording makes abundantly clear, the complicit and colluding Johnson was a spineless pander, colluding with Guppy in what was quite evidently a criminal enterprise, namely causing someone grievous bodily harm.

Johnson was prepared to do Guppy's dirty work in order to allay Guppy's fear about being found out in a serious fraud. Had Guppy 'finished the job', as he euphemistically put it, and had the journalist, Stuart Collier, been murdered, Johnson, being in common law an accessory before the fact, would have faced a hefty jail sentence.

In Johnson's helpfully providing Guppy with Collier's details he had no means of knowing how far Guppy would go but Johnson would doubtless have been familiar with his fellow Bullingdon Club member's frequent boast of being a 'potential psychopath'.[87]

Furthermore Johnson would also have been aware of his great friend's temper. As Guppy puts it in his memoir: 'I had a temper that I could never ignore and that it seemed I was quite capable of hurting someone if I felt they deserved a beating.' [88]

On 24 March 2013, Boris Johnson appeared on the BBC's *Andrew Marr Show* expecting the usual safe PR interview about his aims and achievements only to receive the exact opposite from Marr's stand-in host, Eddie Mair:

'What does that say about you, Boris Johnson?' Mair challenged after he'd raised the Guppy affair. 'Wanting to be a part of someone being physically assaulted? You're a nasty piece of work, aren't you?'

Quite how someone who had got themselves so uncritically involved in the Guppy affair could then present themselves as being in favour of law and order in London while he was standing for mayor or indeed as a Tory MP for Henley and later Uxbridge is a mystery. The answer can only be someone of breathtaking arrogance and entitlement, or of what Aristotle called 'an incontinent personality'.

Given that, according to his biographer, Andrew Gimson, Johnson is prepared to lie about almost anything if it suits his purpose (making, for example, repeated promises of marriage to someone whom he wishes merely to seduce and abandon[89]) his flustered denials of any involvement in the Guppy affair cannot be taken seriously.

Elsewhere when he has been cornered about the tape, Johnson has admitted to this much:

Darius and I had a long rambling conversation that took in many heroes, many military heroes of ours, Rommel...

This excuse prompted a scathing comment on a socialist

blog: 'Rommel! So there you have it, Tory candidate name-checks Nazi as military hero – probably he'd dismiss it as just 'richly comic' but Nazis, to rich and right-wing racists like Johnson are not funny. Even when they play the fool.'[90]

To Johnson's considerable chagrin the Guppy scandal has not and will not go away. When on the TV programme *Have I got News for You*, Ian Hislop of *Private Eye* took Boris Johnson to task over his part in providing Guppy with an address whilst knowing that he might be enabling a crime to be committed, a visibly paling and snarling Johnson stared back at Hislop and seethed apoplectically.

Hislop recalls, 'He was absolutely livid because I brought up the Darius Guppy tape, which I found immensely funny. He was in a terrific strop and blustered about an elephant trap.'[91]

Johnson's intemperate reaction prompts the inevitable question: if nothing had 'eventuated' from the taped conversation and if indeed it was all a joke, then why be so upset by it? – but of course it wasn't so innocent after all and darker deeds were certainly afoot.

MANY OF JOHNSON'S LIES are harmless. He was, for example, asked by *Who's Who* to provide a hobby for his entry. He chose 'scuba-diving'. His first wife, Allegra Mostyn-Owen, pointed out that scuba diving was in fact her hobby, 'which he was rather bad at – I did laugh. He uses up his oxygen too fast. I don't think he ever repeated it [scuba diving], so it was a bit of a fib, but kind of vaguely revealing.'[92]

Other lies however have had a more far-reaching effect. His lie about Jacques Delors and the Maastricht Treaty wishing to castrate every independent country in Europe was splashed all over the front page of the *Sunday Telegraph* but was then also translated into Danish at a moment when Denmark was caught up in the thick of a referendum about its place in Europe.

Johnson's article was to be widely reprinted in Denmark's newspapers. 'My boast,' Johnson proclaimed (with the requisite helping of self-deprecation), 'and I make it in the confidence that no one gives a monkey's, is that I probably did contribute to the Danish rejection of Maastricht.'[93]

It would seem that this was in fact the case. Before the article's appearance opinion polls had suggested a narrow vote in favour of the Maastricht treaty on 2 June; afterwards they pointed to a narrow vote against.

Johnson rejoiced in his article's impact and now recalls: 'With less than a month until the Danish referendum [...] the story was seized on by the No campaign. They photocopied it a thousandfold. They marched the streets of Copenhagen with my story fixed to their banners. And on 2 June, a spectacularly sunny day, they joyously rejected the Treaty and derailed the project. Jacques Delors was not the only victim of the disaster; the aftershocks were felt across Europe and above all in Britain.'[94]

In his book on Brexit, Denis MacShane has outlined the origins of Johnson's duplicitous threats to Europe and to the hidden hand behind them:

> Boris Johnson and the other editors who for more than two decades have published myths, lies and propaganda about Europe could only have acted thus if they had the blessing of their proprietors. In the 1970s, Rupert Murdoch's papers were reasonably honest about Europe and supported the Yes vote in the 1975 referendum. Why and when did he change? His [Murdoch's] latest biographer, David McKnight, is a fellow Australian who published a penetrating biography and political analysis of Murdoch in 2012. According to McKnight:

'The key to Murdoch's line on Europe is not hostility to EU so much as blind pro-Americanism. One of the consistent themes in the political line which he encouraged on the *Times* was that he saw the EU as a rival to the US. He bitterly opposed those Conservatives who want Britain to have a degree of independence and some critical distance from the US.'

Professor McKnight's analysis rings true. It explains why Conrad Black, the neo-conservative Canadian admirer of Ronald Reagan and George W. Bush, who became owner of the *Daily Telegraph* as well as the *Spectator*, which has the biggest circulation of any political weekly in Britain, was also anti-European. Black appointed Boris Johnson editor of the *Spectator* to ensure that Britain's most virulent but very clever anti-European propagandist was at the centre of the London press hostility against the EU.[95]

David Usborne, the Brussels correspondent of the *Independent* said of Johnson, 'Boris understood immediately what the *Telegraph* wanted to hear and he delivered in spades. Once he got his confidence up he started firing every torpedo he had at the Commission. He was writing things without really believing in his heart what he was writing. He would take something that might make a few paragraphs and turn it into an atomic bomb. I don't really think he was pursuing a political agenda about Europe – I think he was pursuing his own future.'[96]

Johnson is also credited with having created a future for UKIP, widely regarded as a retrograde addition to the British body politic:

A spokesman from UKIP (United Kingdom Independence Party), which campaigns for Britain's withdrawal from the EU, says that Boris's writings 'helped to pave' the way for the rise of his party. Its leader Nigel Farage goes further by saying that before Boris made them a fashionable cause, Eurosceptic leanings were 'something that would only be shared amongst close personal friends. They were a minority pursuit.' After Boris, there were few on the Right who did not join the Eurosceptic bandwagon.[97]

Speaking of his self-serving antics in Brussels on the BBC programme *Desert Island Discs* in October 2005 Johnson told his listeners,

> ...everything I wrote from Brussels, I found was sort of chucking these rocks over the garden wall and I listened to this amazing crash from the greenhouse next door over in England as everything I wrote from Brussels was having this amazing, explosive effect on the Tory party, and it really gave me this rather weird sense of power.[98]

Johnson's rapacious power-hunger brings to mind a salutary thought from *The Restaurant at the End of the Universe* by Douglas Adams: 'It is a well-known fact that those people who most want to rule people are, *ipso facto*, those least suited to do it... anyone who is capable of getting themselves made president should on no account be allowed to do the job.'

It is worth noting in passing that the 'explosive' story which Johnson filed ('Delors Plans to Rule Europe') wasn't actually his own. It was merely an exaggerated version of a story which had been filed by John Palmer, the *Guardian*'s Brussels correspondent, a few days before. Palmer still feels 'incensed' by Johnson's plagiarism and by his distortion of the facts.

> ...as a journalist he [Johnson] is thoroughly irresponsible, inventing stories. Just before the Danish referendum, I wrote a story about Delors' thinking on the next stages of political integration in the *Guardian*. Boris came up to me when it

appeared and asked whether I'd seen the relevant documents. He then rewrote my story and completely distorted it to say 'Delors Plans to Rule Europe.'

In fact, it was all about mere *ideas* on majority voting, more powers for the European Parliament and that sort of thing. Then what happened was that the extreme Europhobes in Denmark took Boris's inaccurate version and produced it as a leaflet. Whenever he was challenged about his rubbish, he would never actually defend his corner – he just blamed London, he was quite shameless. But what Boris wrote was taken as gospel by the zealots. It fuelled the whole UKIP phenomenon.

A Boris supporter pointed out to Sonia Purnell, 'The irony is that Boris is a pro-European at heart. So why did he do it? pure opportunism. It made him feel powerful.'[99]

JOHNSON MAY STILL, somewhat deludedly, be thought of in some quarters as a 'national treasure' but he is hardly thought of as one in Liverpool. Shortly after a much-loved Liverpudlian taxi-driver, Ken Bigley, who had courageously been bringing humanitarian aid from Liverpool to Iraq, had been kidnapped by ISIS and publicly decapitated, Johnson commissioned and published a peculiarly tasteless leader in the *Spectator.*

It was a sneering, class-ridden article by Simon Heffer that was signally devoid of empathy and which spitefully accused Liverpudlians of wallowing in their 'victim status'. Liverpool, Johnson's *Spectator* declared, was 'hooked on grief and likes to wallow in a sense of vicarious victimhood'.

It went on to criticise the way Liverpool people had reacted to the capture and murder in Iraq of Ken Bigley and it accused them of 'mawkish sentimentality' in their having been distressed by a Liverpool charity worker's execution at the hands of psychotic killers. The *Spectator*'s leader was, by any standards, gratuitously vile and Johnson's elitist and snobbish hand in the piece was apparent:

> The extreme reaction to Mr Bigley's murder is fed by the fact that he was a Liverpudlian. A combination of economic misfortune…and an excessive predilection for welfarism have created a peculiar and deeply unattractive psyche among many Liverpudlians.[100]

In an increasingly tense situation the wretched Johnson was prevailed upon by his then party leader, Michael Howard to apologise to the people of Liverpool – Howard being anxious not to lose Liverpool's Tory vote, in addition to Howard's having been a long-term supporter of Liverpool's football team.

Johnson was reluctantly bundled off to Liverpool, unclear as to how he should address the city. He would gracelessly nickname the ill-starred venture, 'Operation Scouse-Grovel' but was soon to realise that he was on a very sticky wicket and his embarrassed insincerity was scented out by no less a person than Ken Bigley's brother.

When Johnson appeared on the BBC's Roger Phillips Radio show in Liverpool and when, after a mealy-mouthed apology, Johnson foolishly claimed that he could 'not retract the broad thrust of the article', Paul Bigley saw a red mist and came onto the programme to tell Boris: 'You're a self-centred, pompous twit – even your body language on TV is wrong. You don't look right, never mind act right. Get out of public life!'

As Sonia Purnell, puts it: 'It was a rare occasion when a member of the public has taken Boris on and for a moment he looked shaken by it. 'That was a difficult moment – it stripped a coat off him,' says Quentin Letts, one of the press pack following Boris. "It hasn't happened much."'[101]

JOHNSON'S BIOGRAPHER, Sonia Purnell, has made a particularly unsettling observation of her subject: 'He never laughs. Real laughter involves losing control, and Boris never does that.'

Interestingly it's been shown that the more someone practices self-deception, the less likely they are genuinely to laugh.[102]

Rather than his expressing real laughter, Johnson instead opts for becoming a mere character. In his book *On Becoming a Character* the psychoanalyst Christopher Bollas defines a 'character' as being someone whose deeper self is empty, or angry, or socially alienated.

An Oxford contemporary who was interviewed by Sonia Purnell but who didn't wish to give her name said of him:

> Boris showed then that he was not loyal, that he does not have many real friends, as it is all about him. People were wary of him. He was always fudging everything. So I could see that Boris wouldn't really keep friends because he doesn't have principles. I knew that bumbling thing was an act – he has a real 'economical with the actualité' persona.[103]

Michael Binyon, the *Times* correspondent in Brussels, remembers attending the daily press conferences and being asked by a veteran French journalist present as she indicated Boris Johnson, this shambolic 17-stone British fabulist, 'Qui est ce monstre?'[104]

Curiously, Johnson's former partner in crime, Darius Guppy, has recently stepped forward to comment on the great issue of the day. Margaret Thatcher once said of Boris Johnson, 'He's my favourite journalist'[105] but, writing in the *New Statesman*, Guppy chastises his friend for his reciprocal love of Thatcherism: '…the Boris I knew well at school and university shared with me a love of classics – in particular, the heroes of the classics and the primal values that moved them. While such a world-view is compatible with a love of country, I do not see Achilles or Hector bowing before such a patently ignoble, money-worshipping and ultimately unpatriotic philosophy as Thatcherism.

'Let Johnson and Michael Gove,' he concludes, 'also challenge Washington and Goldman Sachs and then we will see how brave they really are.'[106]

There is no likelihood of this and, as regards Thatcher there is little chance of Johnson being wrenched away from her egregious effigy or legacy. According to Johnson his wife Marina, he has claimed, 'found him sobbing in the street over Thatcher's downfall. Claiming it was as if 'someone had shot Nanny.'[107]

To compare for a moment the difference between a European and a British mind-set: on Thursday 25 February 2016, the European Parliament voted for an EU-wide arms embargo against Saudi in protest against its bombardment of its southern neighbour, Yemen, and the willful killing of civilians and the bombing of schools.

This may be set against David Cameron's visiting the weapons manufacturer, BAE Systems, and against his boasting of his efforts to help sell 'brilliant things' such as Eurofighter Typhoons to Saudi Arabia on the very day the European parliament voted for an arms embargo.[108]

It is unlikely that any such vote would ever be passed in

the British Parliament as it's presently constituted – although it might with Jeremy Corbyn's election as prime minister.

Corbyn has distanced himself from Brexit with its 'little Englander' mentality and its espousal of isolationism, its pride in past imperial power, and its free-market capitalism unfettered by government regulations, especially by what it calls 'foreign governments' in Brussels, and its reluctance to adopt the EU's human rights legislation.

Corbyn has said that he wishes to reform the EU from within and to make it a more socialist bloc. In an article for the *Guardian*, he wrote: 'Labour will be running a positive campaign for the real change we need: to unite opposition to austerity and build a Europe of sustainable growth, jobs and social justice'.[109] And in a speech on 14 April 2016 to Labour supporters, Jeremy Corbyn made it clear that leaving the European Union would, in his words, 'lead to a bonfire of rights'.

> Britain needs to stay in the EU as the best framework for trade, manufacturing and cooperation in 21st century Europe. Tens of billion pounds worth of investment and millions of jobs are linked to our relationship with the EU, the biggest market in the world. In contrast to four decades ago, the EU of today brings together most of the countries of Europe and has developed important employment, environmental and consumer protections.
>
> EU membership has guaranteed working people vital employment rights, including four weeks' paid holiday, maternity and paternity leave, protections for agency workers and health and safety in the workplace. Being in the EU has raised Britain's environmental standards, from beaches to air quality, and protected consumers from rip-off charges.

Despite the British media's demonisation of Corbyn, he remains that *rara avis*, a decent, honest and a principled politician, whereas Brexit's agenda is negative, and doom-laden, and led by an egregious cabal of the self-seeking.

Were Brexit's main advocate, Boris Johnson, to influence the referendum on 23 June 2016 a Brexit victory will have been achieved in large part by deceit, and, perish the thought, were Johnson ever to be elected as prime minister those who will have put him there should be advised to watch out for significant cuts in honesty.

A recent memoir by a former cabinet minister, David Laws, claims that Cameron is 'petrified' of Boris Johnson, the London mayor. According to the *Sunday Times*, the book 'says the prime minister fretted [...] about the EU referendum that 'the only person this will help is Boris Johnson, who is clearly after my job.'[110]

Were any further proof needed of Johnson's amoral and dishonest opportunism it can be gathered from his welcoming party for the phone-hacking mogul Rupert Murdoch to Murdoch's new headquarters at London Bridge.

Sweeping aside the carnage caused by this scheming and conniving monopolist who controls the Fox network, and News Corp, and who holds dominion over much of western media, Johnson chose to greet him with emetic effusions of flattery as a 'wise, benevolent, and far-sighted monarchical figure'.[111]

In Australia Murdoch was notorious for encouraging doorstepping techniques amongst his journo hacks that drove their victims to suicide.[112] Ghoulish and necrotic the elderly leopard may be but he hasn't changed his spots and he now has the added comfort of Boris Johnson kow-towing to him.

Anthony Hilton recently revealed in his column in the

Evening Standard a conversation he once had with Rupert Murdoch about the UK's membership of the European Union. Hilton asked Murdoch why he was so opposed to the EU. 'That's easy,' Murdoch replied, 'when I go into Downing Street, they do what I say; when I go to Brussels they take no notice.'[113]

The thought of Johnson in Downing Street being the lickspittle of his undemocratic and unseen paymaster, Rupert Murdoch, is alarming but Johnson is capable of being just that. When there was a move by Johnson's friends to help him to become the proprietor of the *Spectator* as well as being its editor, he commented, 'Still if the owner is someone other than myself, I am ready to be Vichy-like. I am prepared to praise and flatter shamelessly.'[114]

PERHAPS NOTHING can better demonstrate Johnson's wrongheaded perversity than this quote from his TV series *The Dream of Rome* in which he indulges his peculiar revulsion for the early Christians:

> In their suicidal behaviour, in their belief in an afterlife, and in their rejection of the values of the culture in which they found themselves, the early Christians evoke early comparisons with Islamic suicide bombers of today.[115]

Nothing in the behaviour of early Christians warrants such a comparison, of course. Johnson has allowed his naive infatuation with the swaggering atrocities of ancient Rome to cloud his TV scholarship.

A cursory look at the works of Irenaeus, Celsius, Clement of Alexandria, Athanasius or Origen (given their accounts of the conduct of early Christians before Christianity was ruined by its being commandeered by Rome's Emperor Constantine) would reveal a revolutionary spirit that was communalist, almost wholly vegetarian, anti-authoritarian, and pacifist for its first three hundred years.

The early Christians valued sharing; they despised economic inequality and they told truth to power. They certainly weren't suicide bombers and they weren't Tories either.

In the untiring cause of Brand Boris's aggrandisement, Johnson has recently produced a cuttings job on Winston Churchill of which Nick Cohen would write in the *Spectator:*

> Rather rashly, Boris Johnson published *The Churchill factor: How one man made history* last year. It was without historical merit, or intellectual insight, but Johnson did not intend readers to learn about Churchill. The biography was not a Churchill biography but a Johnson campaign biography, where we were invited to see our hero as Winston redux.
>
> Johnson believes in the advance of Johnson. That's all there is. There's nothing else. Most politicians, and many of the rest of us, are ambitious, of course. But politicians normally hope to advance a cause as they advance themselves. Johnson would have you believe that he is breaking with the establishment, risking all, because of his sincere conviction that we must advance the cause of saving Britain from the European Union.
>
> His colleagues do not believe him. Nicholas Soames called him a liar on Twitter yesterday. Jerry Hayes called him a 'copper-bottomed, hypocritical little shit'. The wonder of it is that they may have been understating the case for the prosecution.[116]

Not unsurprisingly, in his making a case for his own defence Johnson overreaches himself and he has on occasion even confessed to a 'Messiah complex' in terms of his own abilities.[117]

Since historical figures with Messiah complexes often end up causing considerable pain and suffering (*vide* Charles Manson and Adolf Hitler) it might be worth bearing in mind Bishop Tutu's classic admonition, namely that 'the one thing that we learn from history is that we don't learn from history.'

IF JOHNSON were to disappear off the face of the earth it would be hard to assess his legacy. He's perhaps most widely known for the so-called 'Boris Bikes' although they are in fact Barclays Bikes since they are paid for by Barclays Bank. Johnson however has made off with Barclays' credit although the idea for the bikes belonged neither to him nor to Barclays' bank. As Nigel Cawthorne points out, 'Before he had left office, Ken Livingstone had suggested a scheme of street-corner bike hire across the city. These became Boris bikes and he was happy to take credit for them at the 2012 election.'[118]

Despite his ostensible devotion to an environmentally friendly method of transport, Johnson's attempts to make London bike-friendly have failed:

> He came under criticism for his £4-million-a-mile cycling superhighways, which appeared to be nothing more than a line of blue paint that did nothing to protect their users. Indeed two people died at one junction in 2011.[119]

If Johnson is criticised he is liable to throw all his toys out of the pram, and if criticised in print, careless editors who are unaware that Johnson has a thin and notably humourless layer of skin have found themselves in receipt of an email containing the vicious message, 'Fuck off and die.'[120]

Sonia Purnell adds chillingly, 'The wife of one of his Bulling-don Club cohorts at Oxford said that her husband "would not speak about Boris, even off the record, as he is frightened of what he might do back. A lot of people are."'[121]

WITHIN BREXIT, Johnson must qualify as its Alpha Male but he overlooks the fact that for idealistic reasons, the Tory Party's Alpha Male, Winston Churchill, called for a 'United States of Europe' shortly after the end of World War Two – Churchill's thought was that such a unity could provide a bulwark against any further devastation in Europe.

Brexit seeks to undo that unity and it's led by a cadre of conservatives who protest their love of country with a self-satisfied zeal and yet who are unable to conserve the quality of its air, nor of its soil nor of its water. They are largely climate change deniers, advocates of nuclear power and nuclear weapons, proponents of genetically modified foods and those who give polluters a free rein if it 'serves the economy'. They will defend slave wages and the iniquities of 'zero hours contracts' and the privatisation of the National Health Service by rapacious US con men, while they fight with a low cunning to conserve a depraved British body-politic based upon an unconscionable disparity between untold wealth and unspeakable poverty and upon the idle values of transient celebrity.

In a peculiar twist to the Brexit saga, Rupert Murdoch's newspaper, the *Sun*, tried to convey the impression that the richest woman in the world was opposed to Europe and that she'd launched forth at a luncheon held at Windsor Castle into a 'venomous' tirade against all things European, saying 'I don't understand Europe' and that Europe was, in her words, 'going in the wrong direction.'

Her Majesty let rip at the then Deputy PM during a lunch at Windsor Castle, the *Sun* has been told.

The 89-year-old monarch firmly told passionate pro-European Mr Clegg that she believed the EU was heading in the wrong direction.

The queen is said to have snapped back angrily: 'I don't understand Europe.'

A parliamentary source, who relayed the remark to the *Sun*, said: 'It was said with quite some venom and emotion. I shall never forget it.'

Michael Gove was also present and it is suspected that it was he who leaked the story.

The *Sun* continued:

The claims will explode a furious controversy. Brexit-backing Tory MPs are already leaping on the *Sun*'s revelations as a strong sign the queen is secretly on the side of 'Leave' ahead of the landmark EU referendum on June 23. But British monarchs are deemed to be above politics and have always tried hard to stay out of divisive issues. The upcoming EU referendum is one of the most divisive in decades, splitting the country down the middle on whether to remain or leave.[122]

Following the queen's outburst, the Palace declined to comment on what it called 'spurious, anonymously sourced claims' and insisted that 'the queen remains politically neutral, as she has for 63 years.'

This, of course, is not the case. To give but two examples: the queen played a part in Australia's left-wing prime minister, Gough Whitlam, being replaced though the back-channel instructions which she issued to her governor general, Sir John Kerr, and she also made her views known before the Scottish referendum, thus quashing the hopes of independent minded Scots having a country free from being ruled by Westminster and also perhaps freed from the archaic practice of having a hereditary monarch as its head of state.

However much the Palace may stick to the conceit that the queen is above politics, the Eurosceptic members of the queen's Privy Council (her special advisers) who were lunching with her that day at Windsor Castle could well have taken the view that she should see Europe as a threat to her sovereignty since Europeans are more inclined to elect their heads of state rather than, as in the UK, to have the office imposed on them by archaic tradition.[123]

When Christopher Hitchens adopted the United States as his country he was in the habit of boasting that it was 'the only country based on an idea'. But Europe can cap that being a whole continent based on an idea; possibly a set of rather good ideas.

In the words of Douglas Adams: 'To be frank, it sometimes seems that the American idea of freedom has more to do with my freedom to do what I want than your freedom to do what you want. I think that, in Europe, we're probably better at understanding how to balance those competing claims, though not a lot.'

In a recent fit of megalomania, Boris Johnson told the *Times* that he liked the idea of being a 'plucky individual' standing up to the evils of the European Union. During the course of an interview, Johnson took pains to point out to his interviewer that *Spectre*, the most recent Bond movie, had been partly shot in his mayor of London offices. 'You are in the place,' Johnson boasted, 'where James Bond shoots the evil baddie who is hell bent on subverting democracy around the world through a supra-national organisation... I think there's a metaphor there.'[124]

Johnson may, somewhat pitifully, persuade himself that he is a reincarnation of James Bond but perhaps there's a more apt metaphor to be found in his current designs on William Blake.

Blake is buried in Bunhill Fields, a quiet haven in the centre of London which Boris Johnson – ever anxious to curry favour with city planners and profiteers – is determined to overshadow with an oppressive cluster of towering office blocks.

Blake's grave is the last resting place of a man who represented all that's best in the English spirit: a man who was horrified by the thought that 'commerce settles on every tree.'

In the words of Niall McDevitt, the principal campaigner against the multi-storey development 'He [Johnson] will be remembered as the mayor who sold London's skyline.'

McDevitt is not alone in his view. Writing in the *Observer*, Rowan Moore, the author of *Slow Burn City: London in the Twenty-First Century*, urges his readers to pity Johnson's successor as Johnson prepares to leave City Hall for they'll be 'faced with ill-planned developments and vanity projects', in other words 'the bloated, bulging, light-blocking buildings' that Johnson leaves in his wake.

Moore points out that Johnson's phalanxes of towers that cast swathes of land 'into almost permanent shadow' are ultimately 'bad for business and bad for the London brand, promoting as it does both a speculative bubble and shoddy products'.

Moore finally bids *adieu* to the much-vaunted classicist with these humiliating words: 'Goodbye Boris. You have not left your city, as the Ephebic oath required of Athenians, more beautiful than you found it. You have been more like Nero, fiddling with vanity projects while it burns with clumsy over-development.'[125]

McDevitt has written an open letter to Johnson:

Dear Mayor,

I have started an AVAAZ petition to ask you to rethink your approval of the development at Bunhill Fields. It has been rushed through too fast. It is going to be one of your more unpopular decisions and may bounce back to haunt you as you begin to seek higher rungs of power than the one you already occupy.

A huge development going up at the side of this beloved green space and cultural heritage site will affect it negatively in numerous ways, some temporarily, some permanently. In the short term the noise and disruption will be a blight on this oasis of tranquillity. In the long term, the eleven and ten storey blocks will make Bunhill Fields colder and darker, oppressing the open space and ruining the skyline. Campaigners such as the Ancient Monuments Society have already warned you that the project is a 'bullying' and 'overwhelming' one.'

Johnson did not reply.

When Blake was thirteen he wrote a poem called *Song*, about Phoebus who catches a bird in a silver net, shuts it in a golden cage and mocks its 'loss of liberty'. Later Blake would take the radical, anti-capitalist view that 'where any view of Money exists Art cannot be carried on, but war only.' Blake thus nailed Bullinger Toryism and its crass devotion to high finance and the military-industrial complex in a couple of phrases.

By contrast Johnson's loquacious, blustering claims to love England (and, via Brexit, to be protecting all that is best about it) are fraudulent; his monomaniac plans to foist himself further and further upon the body-politic are disturbing and to Blake aficionados Johnson's imminent plan to cast his oafish shadow upon Blake's mortal remains and to deprive them of light is akin to blasphemy.

However, while Johnson may be a cult figure to some of his fellow Tories, there are growing signs that his excesses are too much for others. At the time of writing, the former Conservative MP and aide to Margaret Thatcher, Matthew Parris, launched a scathing attack on the pro-Brexit mayor, denouncing him for alleged 'dishonesty, vacuity, sexual impropriety and veiled homophobia'.

'Somebody has to call a halt to the gathering pretence that if only you're sufficiently comical in politics you can laugh everything off,' Parris wrote. 'Incompetence is not funny. Policy vacuum is not funny. A careless disregard for the truth is not funny. Advising old mates planning to beat someone up is not funny. Abortions and gagging orders are not funny. Creeping ambition in a jester's cap is not funny. Vacuity posing as merriment, cynicism posing as savviness, a wink and a smile covering for betrayal... these things are not funny.'

Parris describes the mayor as a 'lacklustre' politician, and claims that Johnson was unable to defend his recent claims about the European Union in front of the Treasury select committee in Parliament. Andrew Tyrie, the committee chair, accused Johnson of 'exaggerating to the point of misrepresentation'. It was not the case, as Johnson had maintained, that the EU had banned the British from recycling teabags or that children under eight had been prevented from blowing up balloons. Nor had the EU regulated on the size of coffins and nor were EU regulations costing Britain £600m a day.

Parris added: 'But there's a pattern to Boris's life, and it isn't the lust for office, or for applause, or for susceptible women, that mark out this pattern in red warning ink. It's the casual dishonesty, the cruelty, the betrayal; and, beneath the betrayal, the emptiness of real ambition: the ambition to do anything useful with office once it is attained.'[126]

The writer Will Black wittily quipped in a tweet addressed to the mayor:

Hi @*MayorofLondon* do you think Matthew Parris should be beaten up for this?

Again, no reply from Johnson's office was forthcoming.

Hot on the heels of Parris, and clearly alarmed by the possibility that Johnson could become Britain's prime minister, the veteran political commentator, Nick Cohen, entitled an article for the *Guardian*, 'Boris Johnson. Liar, conman – and prime minister?'

He warned, 'It is easy to see how Boris Johnson could be prime minister by the autumn. 'Leave' wins, and David Cameron resigns. We already know that a majority of the 140,000 or so Conservative party members, who will decide the government of a country of 64 million, back him. Give them the chance, and they will put him in Downing Street.'

Cohen indicates that Johnson's attitude toward Europe has been entirely opportunistic. 'Any man,' Cohen says, 'with a functioning sense of shame would have worried about his long record of supporting the EU. As late as February, Johnson was saying that leaving would embroil "the government for several years in a fiddly process of negotiating new arrangements, so diverting energy from the real problems of this country". And so it would. Elsewhere he acknowledged that we would not get free trade without accepting EU regulation and immigration.'

Cohen points out that 'the mayor of London has been treated with woozy indulgence by the media. My supposedly hard-bitten colleagues have bought his persona as a lovable card, and ignored the emptiness beneath. But Britain may pay the price.'[127]

However it's not just Britain that may pay the price, it's also Europe – if not the world.

NOTES

1   'He has something of the night about him', Ann Widdecombe, May
     1997.

2   Ann Widdecombe, *Strictly Ann*, Weidenfeld & Nicolson, http://
     www.dailymail.co.uk/news/article-2330986/The-wrath-Widdy-
     Ann-Widdecombe-brands-Michael-Howard-gloating-bully-blasts-
     Cameron-obsessed-image-explosive-new-book.html

3   Andrew Anthony, 'Howard's way', *Observer*, 27 March 2005.

4   BBC News, 'Experts in international law have criticised Tory leader
     Michael Howard's stance on the Iraq war as "unlawful"'. Friday,
     29 April, 2005, http://news.bbc.co.uk/1/hi/uk_politics/vote_2005/
     frontpage/4497777.stm

5   http://www.dailymail.co.uk/news/article-3198829/How-Michael-
     Howard-got-entangled-slew-doubtful-companies.html

6   ibid.

7   Neil Clark, 'A David Cameron government would be brimming with
     hawks', *Week*, June 29 2009.

8   Richard Garner, 'What is it about Michael Gove that makes people
     hate him so much? No Education Secretary has ever embarked on such
     radical reform, so quickly, since Kenneth Baker', *Independent*, 9 April
     2012.

9   Anthony Horowitz, 'I always defended Michael Gove. Then I met
     him: My fellow children's writers hate the Education Secretary. Now I
     finally understand why', the *Spectator*, 15 March 2014.

10   *Daily Telegraph*, 26 June 2009.

11   Bill Blanko, 'Ah, an expenses free-for-all – just like old times. Bill
     Blanko looks back fondly on an era when journalists could claim almost
     as wildly as MPs', *Guardian*, 14 May 2009.

12   Isabel Oakeshott, 'Gadzooks, Boris admits bumbling is a cunning plan',
     Sunday Times, 14 April 2013.

13   Simon Heffer, The Guest Column, *New Statesman*, 4-10 March.

14   *Observer*, 5 October 2003.

15   *Daily Telegraph*, 16 February 1996.

16   *Spectator*, 2 February 2002.

17   ibid.

18   ibid. 16 November 2002.

19   ibid. 11 January 2003.

20   ibid. 24 February 2001, cf Sonia Purnell, op. cit. p. 193.

21   Nigel Cawthorne, *Blond Ambition: The Rise and Rise of Boris Johnson*,
     Endeavour Press, 2015, p. 50.

22   Cawthorne, op. cit. p. 55.

23   Sonia Purnell, *Just Boris: A Tale of Blond Ambition*, Aurum Press, 2011,
     p. 342.

24   Denis MacShane, *Brexit: How Britain Will Leave Europe*, I.B.Tauris,
     2015, p. 207.

25   Dennis Rahkonen, 'Each Day, Capitalism Kills far more Innocents
     Than Died on 9/11', *Dissident Voice*, 3 April 2009.

26   Ronald Reagan, 1981.

27   '...as a cyclist I think pedestrians are the most dangerous features on
     the road at the moment.' Boris Johnson on the Jeremy Vine Show on
     BBC Radio 2, cf. Richard Hebditch, 'Pedestrians and pedallers unite!

Cyclists and pedestrians need to work together to improve the streets of London', *Guardian*, 12 March 2008.

28   Darren Johnson, 'The overall number of road casualties has gone up by 5 per cent under Boris Johnson', *Left Foot Forward.*

29   Purnell, op. cit. p. 171.

30   ibid, p. 239.

31   *Daily Telegraph*, 26 February 2004.

32   Boris Johnson, *Lend Me Your Ears*, Harper Collins, 2004, p. 317.

33   Boris Johnson, *Have I Got Views for You*, Harper Collins, 2008, p. 272.

34   Leader entitled 'Infantile resentment' in *Spectator*, 22 November 2003, p. 7.

35   Andrew Gimson, *Boris: The Rise of Boris Johnson*, Simon and Schuster, 2012, p. 98.

36   Gimson, op. cit. p. 93.

37   Simon Hoggart, 'Boris Johnson has been brought to his knees by a man who died in 1312' *Guardian*, 25 March 2013.

38   Peter Walker, 'Boris Johnson: Eddie Mair did "a splendid job"' *Guardian*, 25 March 2013.

39   Cawthorne, op. cit. p. 29.

40   Gimson, op. cit. p. 57.

41   MacShane, op. cit. p. 174.

42   ibid. p. 172-3.

43   Boris Johnson, The Annual Margaret Thatcher Lecture, 27 November 2013.

44   Boris Johnson, 'There's a simple solution to this Euro-elections sham', *Daily Telegraph*, 27 April 2014.

45 Purnell, op. cit. p. 201.

46 ibid. p. 43.

47 ibid. p. 395.

48 ibid. pp 386-7.

49 According to Nigel Cawthorne, *Blond Ambition: The Rise and Rise of Boris Johnson*, this has now risen to £500,000 p. a.

50 Purnell, op. cit. p. 73.

51 ibid. p. 72.

52 ibid. p. 73.

53 ibid. pp. 340, 341.

54 Gimson, op. cit. pp. 68-9.

55 ibid. pp. 68-9.

56 ibid. pp. 74-5.

57 Purnell, op. cit. p. 69.

58 Gimson, op. cit. p. 259.

59 Simon Walters, 'Boris, Petsy and a "pyramid of piffle"', *Mail on Sunday*, 7 November 2004, p. 7. 'I have not had an affair with Petronella. It is complete balderdash. It is an inverted pyramid of piffle. It is all completely untrue and ludicrous conjecture. I am amazed people can write this drivel.'

60 Purnell, op. cit. p. 261.

61 Gimson, op. cit. p. 407.

62 Michael Wolff, 'The Boris Show', *Vanity Fair*, 29 April 2008.

63 Boris Johnson, 'Killing deer to save them,' *Daily Telegraph*, 9 July 1997 and re-published in *Lend Me Your Ears*, Harper Perennial, 2004.

64   ABJ stands for Alexander Boris Johnson and an Oppidan (lit. town-dweller) which is the name of the fee-paying Eton students who live in boarding houses in the town of Eton – as distinct from the Eton Scholars who live in the college buildings. The Wall Game is often played between Oppidans and Scholars who wear gowns and are known as 'Tugs', being short for togati or gown-wearers. Johnson was a 'tug'.

65   Gimson, op. cit. p. 55.

66   Barney Ronay, 'Oxbridge and elitism: Young, rich and drunk. The Bullingdon Club draws its all-male members by secret ballot from Oxford University's social elite.' Barney Ronay explains the raucous rituals that unite this band of yobbish toffs, *Guardian*, 9 May 2008.

67   ibid.

68   Evelyn Waugh, *Brideshead Revisited*, London: Chapman and Hall, 1927; Penguin Books, 2001, p. 7.

69   Waugh, op. cit. p. 8.

70   Joy Lo Dico 'The Sikorski set: the Polish foreign minister has locked horns with Cameron – but their history goes back to the Bullingdon Club.' Joy Lo Dico traces an Establishment power clique from the Bullingdon Club to Brussels, *Evening Standard*, 26 June 2014.

71   Ronay, op. cit. p. 117.

72   Tom McTague, 'Bullingdon Club initiation ceremony claim: New members of David Cameron's old club 'burn £50 note in front of beggar.' A friend of one of the exclusive club's super-wealthy members revealed the sick prank to an Oxford student newspaper', *Daily Mirror*, 23 February 2013.

73   Boris Johnson, 'In Defence of Public Schools,' *Eton Chronicle*, 12 December 1980.

74   *Evening Standard*, 19 January 2010, cited by Purnell, op. cit. p. 401.

75 'When Boris Met Dave,' Channel 4, docudrama, October 2009.

76 I am indebted to Martin Soames for this reaction to the Bullingdon Club photograph in a private communication.

77 Gimson, op. cit. p. 117.

78 Darius Guppy, *Roll the Dice: A True Saga of Love, Money and Betrayal*, Blake Publishing, 1996, p. 102.

79 The audio is available on Soundcloud and the transcript is available here: http://boris-johnson.blogspot.co.uk/search/label/darius%20guppy

80 http://www.whatnextjournal.org.uk/Pages/Politics/Boris2.html

81 http://www.dailymail.co.uk/news/article-1167172/The-high-society-psycho-come-haunt-Boris-Johnson.html#ixzz41OAMeLLB

82 Transmitted 24 March 2013 on BBC2.

83 http://www.dailymail.co.uk/news/article-2361999/Boris-Johnsons-friend-Darius-Guppy-admits-horrifying-attack-journalist-insulted-wife.html#ixzz41NP8My5r

84 http://www.dailymail.co.uk/news/article-2361999/Boris-Johnsons-friend-Darius-Guppy-admits-horrifying-attack-journalist-insulted-wife.html#ixzz41nVSzEri *Daily Mail* Reporter 12 July 2013.

85 http://www.telegraph.co.uk/news/celebritynews/9961473/Darius-Guppy-That-element-of-madness-was-always-there.html

86 Darius Guppy, 'Who will bully the bullies?' *New Statesman*, 11 July 2013.

87 Andy McSmith, 'Darius, Boris and a blast from the past: A convicted fraudster and self-confessed 'potential psychopath', Darius Guppy has long been a source of embarrassment for his old friend, Boris Johnson. Now a tape has come to light in which the pair discuss beating up a journalist', *Independent*, 30 March 2009 http://www.dailymail.co.uk/

news/article-2361999/Boris-Johnsons-friend-Darius-Guppy-admits-horrifying-attack-journalist-insulted-wife.html#ixzz41I8sn18i

88   Guppy, op. cit. p. 3.

89   cf Purnell, op. cit.

90   *Socialist Unity*, http://socialistunity.com/boris-johnson-on-law-and-order/

91   Purnell, op. cit. p. 176.

92   Gimson, op. cit. p. 108.

93   ibid, p. 104.

94   *Daily Telegraph*, 15 September 2003.

95   MacShane, p. 175.

96   Gimson, op. cit. p. 99.

97   Purnell, op. cit. p. 115.

98   BBC , 20 October 2005.

99   Purnell, op. cit. p. 128.

100   Leader 'Bigley's fate. We have lost our sense of proportion about what constitutes a tragedy.' *Spectator*, 16 October 2004.

101   Purnell, op. cit. pp. 254-5.

102   Robert F. Lynch, Robert L. Trivers, 'Self-deception inhibits laughter.' *Personality and Individual Differences*, Special Issue on Behavioral genetic contributions to research on individual differences, Volume 53, Issue 4, Elsevier, September 2012, Pages 491-495.

103   Purnell, op. cit. p. 88.

104   Gimson, op. cit. p. 101.

105 Her remark was made to Sir Eric Anderson, Johnson's former Headmaster, Gimson, op .cit. p. 104.

106 Darius Guppy, 'My old friend Boris is wrong on Brexit', *New Statesman*, 4-10 March 2016.

107 *Daily Telegraph*, 15 September 2003; cf. also Purnell op. cit, p. 120.

108 Rowena Mason, political correspondent: David Cameron boasts of 'brilliant' UK arms exports to Saudi Arabia, *Guardian*, 25 February 2016.

109 Jeremy Corbyn, 'Cameron's deal is the wrong one: but Britain must stay in Europe.' 'Opinion', *Guardian*, 20 February 2016.

110 Tim Shipman, Political Editor, 'Palace fights to save Queen's independence: Brexit row has damaged her, admit courtiers.' *Sunday Times*, March 13 2016.

111 Arif Durrani: Boris Johnson welcomes 'benevolent' Murdoch and News UK to London Bridge, *Media Week*, 17 September 2014 .

112 Richard Neville, 'The Life and Crimes of a Global Goebbels', *Counterpunch*, September 1 2006.

113 Anthony Hilton, 'Stay or go – the lack of solid facts means it's all a leap of faith', *Evening Standard*, 25 February 2016.

114 Michael Wolff, The Boris Show, *Vanity Fair*, April 29 2008.

115 Boris Johnson, *The Dream of Rome*, with new material on the rise of Islam, Harper Perennial, 2007, p. 188.

116 Nick Cohen, 'Boris Johnson: Everything about you is phoney', *Spectator*, 22 February 2016.

117 *Evening Standard*, 9 April 2010.

118 Cawthorne, op. cit. p. 114.

119 ibid, p. 118.

120   Purnell op. cit. p. 7.

121   ibid.

122   *Sun*, 9 March 2016; http://www.timescolonist.com/news/world/
       tabloid-claims-queen-wants-u-k-out-of-european-union-palace-
       complains-1.2193715#sthash.8OqSTjLc.dpuf

123   http://www.theguardian.com/media/greenslade/2016/mar/09/its-
       just-possible-that-the-suns-queen-backs-brexit-story-is-true

124   Jack Hill 'You are in the place where James Bond shoots the evil
       baddie', *Times*, 27 February 2016.

125   Rowan Moore, 'Boris Johnson's dire legacy for London.' *Observer*,
       10 April 2016.

126   Matthew Parris, 'Tories have got to end their affair with Boris.'
       Times, 26 March 2016.

127   Nick Cohen, 'Boris Johnson. Liar, conman – and prime minister?'
       Guardian, 26 March 2016.

The Magic of Heathcote Williams

Francis Wyndham

I SOMETIMES ARGUE with my friend Heathcote Williams about his use of pornography as a means of attacking his political enemies. It seems to me an irrelevant weapon in any context, and in the hands of a man with Heathcote's anarchistic, optimistic, nearly utopian convictions it becomes puzzlingly inconsistent. His polemical essays have been appearing, often unsigned, in the underground press over the past decade, and a selection, entitled *Severe Joy*, is listed for publication next year by John Calder. They abound in fantastic, and often very funny, descriptions of the people he disapproves of (such as Mrs Thatcher, Enoch Powell, Ian Paisley, the Royal Family and Jesus Christ) engaged in eccentric forms of sexual intercourse. One might almost assume from a few of these scatological diatribes that he thought there was something intrinsically disgusting and automatically degrading about physical love – and yet the opposite is the case. After all, he was a leading light at the Wet Dream Film Festival organised by *Suck* magazine in Amsterdam nine years ago, and I have heard him express the belief that human sperm contains psychedelic properties. To quote from the 278-year-old hero of his play *The Immortalist*: 'One of the purposes of love-making (not that you can make love – love *is*) is to achieve immortality... When it fails, you get conception.' This seems to imply, in its paradoxical fashion, that Heathcote sees the act of copulation as potentially mystical, perhaps even sacred. So why the emphasis on obscenity as a form of abuse? Isn't there some element of contradiction here? But my argument gets nowhere. Heathcote scowls prettily, tosses what can only be called his 'unruly curls', accuses me of being an irredeemable media turd and a closet Monarchist.

The Immortalist is a wildly stimulating, mildly disturbing duologue in the form of a television interview with a man who refuses to die.

> With the exception of myself and a few others of my ilk still circulating, every human being ever born on this planet has been murdered, consented to be murdered and spent their entire lives preparing for that pointless little spurt so beloved by footling existentialists. It's time for Life and Death to get divorced, maybug. What is more revolutionary than the conquest of death? Marxist-Leninist misery? Property is theft? I bet you two shillings to a toffee apple Proudhon couldn't nick a packet of spam out of Safeways.

I first read it two years ago, when Heathcote called round to see me with a typescript copy. On leaving my house, he was immediately arrested by two policewomen who (he claims) duffed him up and accused him of being drunk in charge of a bicycle. I found myself a key defence-witness at his trial, a long-drawn-out and solemn affair at the end of which he was acquitted. I first saw it acted a year later at the National Theatre of Frestonia – the name given to two streets in North Kensington which, threatened with demolition, had declared a sort of UDI in the manner of *Passport to Pimlico*. It has since been performed in various places, most recently at last month's Edinburgh Festival.

Visitors to the Festival also had the chance of seeing Heathcote play the part of Prospero in a film version of *The Tempest* directed by Derek Jarman. 'Isn't that bit about me breaking my staff and drowning my book supposed to be rather important?' he asked me. 'Well, Derek said he had trouble fitting it into his conception of the play and I think it's been cut.' Nonetheless, Heathcote's performance was praised in the *Listener* as 'melancholically smouldering' – and he might indeed be considered a kind of Prospero to the alternative society (although his personality contains a touch of Ariel's volatility, too, with possibly just a dash of Caliban's balefulness). Since his startling debut in 1964, when he was only 23 and his brilliant book *The Speakers* attracted the admiration of Harold Pinter, William Burroughs, Anthony Burgess, V.S. Pritchett and more, he has gradually achieved the status of super-wizard in a community of nomads, pilgrims and seekers after truth. For two years he successfully ran the Ruff, Tuff, Cream Puff Estate Agency (founded by Wat Tyler in 1381) which advised the homeless on suitable premises to squat. (I remember being taken aback, on receiving the agency's bulletin, to find my brother's house listed in it with the sinister comment: 'No apparent security between 11 and 12 p.m.') Soberly cycling round his domain in Notting Hill, surrounded by the peeling remnants of his own 'wall paintings' (graffiti which have long been accepted by local residents as permanent landmarks – 'Squat now while stocks last,' 'A woman without a man is like a fish without a bicycle'), Heathcote seems to occupy the centre of a charmed circle.

His relationship to 'magic' is of two kinds. He is a skilled conjuror whose tricks have diverted many a geriatric ward (although an attempt to levitate his daughter China on the stage of the Lyttelton Theatre was less successful, and a defiant stab at fire-eating landed him with severe burns in a hospital bed beside a patient with gangrene of the testicles). But he is also receptive to magic in its more literal sense, apparently willing to believe in almost anything, from UFOs to the fairy photos that fooled Conan Doyle. With his Kirlian Camera he has photographed the aura of a 50p piece (Heathcote is no friend to metrication) and found that it resembles a congealed bat's fart. His restless intelligence makes him impatient with logic and he is drawn to overstatement by a genuine indignation mixed with a teasing sense of farce; he celebrates the irrational in a facetiously punning language with evangelical and apocalyptic overtones.

> Clean your spark-plugs, Nosferatu Nerdniks. Ye that are heavy-laden, rip off your clothes, rise up and bathe the world in light. The Recording Angel's got a polaroid. Where's the Kirlian clapper boy? Akashic flashers, unsheathe your auric fronds and let it all hang out so far you gotta pump air into it. Click. Click. Take *infinity*!… Crown King Thing. The aura bomb has been detonated. Our energy is continuous and immortal…

And so on – when he hits this vein, Heathcote can keep it up indefinitely. But in his best work – *The Speakers*, and four of his plays – the whimsical gift of the gab is disciplined by a basic sense of dramatic structure to produce an effect combining lethal accuracy of recorded speech with vertiginous imaginative flights. His study of the Hyde Park orators might have been taken as a masterly piece of reportage when it came out 15 years ago; rereading it today, one can more easily recognise in it the germs of an exuberant creative gift. The critics who praised it so highly were far-seeing: it still has the staying power of a classic. (A dramatised version, staged in 1974, was worthy of the original.) Heathcote's first play, *The Local Stigmatic* (1965), is a short, chilling drama about two drop-outs obsessed to the point of unbalance by the media's fabrication of phoney celebrities; they recognise a minor actor in a pub, follow him out and savagely beat him up. This theme is elaborated in *AC/DC* (1970), a full-length play of dazzling invention and overwhelming power. Both works, considered obscure and unnecessarily violent by many people at the time, now seem to have been uncannily prophetic of the Manson murders. 'What were the Manson murders about?' said Heathcote in an interview.

> You could say they were about somebody trying to get his songs published: a grub under the blanket of the Great Society. The explanation is that there are two tribes: those who are undernourished in terms of tribal approval, and those who are so overnourished that they become severely debilitated... The point is that Attention is a basic human need like food or sex. No child develops without it, and if you don't get it you wrinkle up. And as the media stand now .0001 per cent of the population is getting *crème brûlée* every day, and the rest are being ignored.

In *AC/DC* Heathcote furthered the investigation into the speech rhythms and thought patterns of schizophrenia which he had begun with the character of MacGuinness in *The Speakers*, unnervingly relating paranoid delusions of 'electronic control' to the actual developments in technological progress which underpin our lives. Ending with a trepanation scene performed onstage, it is a very frightening play, and perhaps it frightened Heathcote. Certainly *Hancock's Last Half Hour* (1977) – a witty, melancholy monologue leading up to the comedian's suicide in an Australian hotel-room – reverts to a more humanist theatrical tradition, while *The Immortalist* recalls the dialectical device exploited by Diderot in *Le Neveu de Rameau*.

Since 1970, Heathcote's serious writing for the theatre has become marginally mellower in tone while his propaganda pieces grow more outrageously scabrous. At the time when he was inveighing against famous people as psychic capitalists getting their astral projection on the cheap, he fell in love with the most famous model in the world, Jean Shrimpton, and lived with her for several years. I assume that this item of personal history may be mentioned without impertinence, because Heathcote has published, next to a mutilated photograph of Jean, a virulent exercise in loathing called *Polythene Pam* which rivals Céline's lunatic ravings against the Jews in its intemperate nastiness. It is clear that what Heathcote hated was himself for ever having paused from hating what she represented.

So he is a creature of extremes. Of conventional upper-middle-class origin (educated at Eton, father a QC – 'just like Rumpole', mother a clergyman's daughter), he excels at writing about alcoholics, schizophrenics, junkies, tramps. Accidentally contemporary with such movements as flower power and the drug culture, he became in a sense their Savonarola, embracing their cause with a passion, energy and rigour conspicuously lacking in their other devotees. Possessed of a remarkable intellect, he takes a perverse pleasure in giving credence to the most far-fetched rubbish he can find. Gentle and generous in life, he can be spiteful and violent in print. By the same token, endearingly muddled as a companion, he can rise in his plays to heights of piercing illumination that make one think of Rimbaud.

Originally published in vol. 1 no. 1 of the *London Review of Books*, 25 October 1979

CONTRIBUTORS

Jeremy Harding is a contributing editor at the *LRB*, and the author of *The Uninvited: Refugees at the Rich Man's Gate* and *Mother Country: A Memoir*.

Heathcote Williams, who died in 2017, was a poet, playwright, essayist, lyricist, actor, artist, magician and political agitator. His books include *Whale Nation*, *Autogeddon* and *Royal Babylon*. As an actor he appeared in films including *The Tempest*, *Wish You Were Here* and *Orlando*.

Francis Wyndham, author, editor, man of letters and mentor to writers including Bruce Chatwin, Alan Hollinghurst, V.S. Naipaul, Jean Rhys and Edward St Aubyn, died in 2017.

ABOUT THE 'LRB'

The *London Review of Books* is Europe's leading magazine of culture and ideas. Published twice a month, it provides a space for some of the world's best writers to explore a wide variety of subjects in exhilarating detail – from art and politics to science and technology via history and philosophy, fiction and poetry. In the age of the long read, the *LRB* remains the pre-eminent exponent of the intellectual essay, admired around the world for its fearlessness, its range and its elegance.

As well as book reviews and reportage, each issue also contains poems, reviews of exhibitions and movies, 'short cuts', letters and a diary, and is available in print, online, and offline via our app. Subscribers enjoy unlimited access to every piece we've published since 1979, the year the magazine was founded, in our digital archive. It contains all of the articles in this volume, and many more that might have made the cut. Our website (www.lrb.co.uk) also features a regular blog, podcasts and short documentaries, plus video highlights from our events programme on both sides of the Atlantic, and at the London Review Bookshop.

A reader recently described the *LRB* as 'the best thing about being a human'. Make it the highlight of your fortnight, too, by taking out a subscription: www.lrb.me/beast